For the Kids 2!

For the Kids 2!

The Revised and Updated Family-Friendly Guide to Outings and Activities for Children in Ireland

Compiled and Edited by
The Liffey Press

Published by The Liffey Press
Ashbrook House, 10 Main Street
Raheny, Dublin 5, Ireland
www.theliffeypress.com

A catalogue record of this book is
available from the British Library.

ISBN 1-904148-85-9

Printed in Spain by Graficas Cems

Contents

Preface

The Liffey Press is delighted to be publishing this revised and updated edition of *For the Kids 2!: A Family-Friendly Guide to Outings and Activities for Children in Ireland*. The first edition of this book was very favourably received by parents, teachers and others, and we hope you will find this updated edition, with 66 new entries, both interesting and useful.

The descriptions of the outings and activities in these pages came from a variety of sources and we would first like to thank all the individual organisations that responded to our questionnaire and sent information to us. We are also grateful to Heritage Ireland, the OPW, Fáilte Ireland, the Environment and Heritage Service (NI), the National Trust (NI) and the many local tourism boards that provided useful information about attractions to be included in the book.

We have made every attempt for the information in *For the Kids 2!* to be accurate and up-to-date, but inevitably some dates, costs or other details may change and we advise the reader to contact individual organisations directly to confirm that the information is correct. Also, because this book is designed as a directory, not as a guidebook, we can accept no responsibility for the accuracy of the descriptions provided or of the quality of the activities on offer.

We apologise to any organisations that may have been inadvertently overlooked in this guidebook and advise them to send us appropriate information for consideration for the next edition (see booking form at the back of the book). We would also welcome receipt of any corrections and updates from organisations listed in the book so that future printings will be as accurate as possible.

To the individuals who contributed short essays to this book — Sean Connor, Beatrice Kelly, Paddy Madden, Catherine O'Connell, Helen O'Donoghue and Darina Shouldice — a heartfelt thank you. Your thoughts and advice on how to keep children fully engaged with the world around them add considerable value to an already useful publication.

Finally, we would be very grateful for any recommendations, comments or ideas about how to make future editions of this book even more useful. We look forward to hearing from you.

David Givens
Publisher
May 2006

Note on the layout:
The listings in this book are organised alphabetically by province, by county within the province and again by organisation within the county. There is a complete index at the back of the book as well as an index by type of activity. Symbols used throughout the book to show what facilities are available include:

🍽 for café/restaurant/coffee shop;

♿ for facilities for the disabled;

🚻 for public toilets;

🎁 for gift shop.

We would recommend, however, that readers telephone in advance to verify that specific facilities are available.

To Sam and Luke

To Christopher, Holly and Faye

To Ann

For the Kids in Connaught

Athenry Arts and Heritage Centre

The Square, Athenry, Co Galway
Tel: 091-844661   Fax: 091-850674
info@athenryheritagetown.com

- Open April to October, Monday to Friday, 10.00 to 4.00; tours can be arranged outside these times
- Adults, €5.00; Students, €4.00; Family, €15.00
- Located in the centre of Athenry
- Caters for children's parties
- Caters for school groups/tours
- Special programmes for children

Athenry is a picturesque and historical town located in the west of Ireland. It is the only walled town left in Ireland or Britain whose still-intact medieval walls are clearly visible to the approaching visitor. Athenry was the first town in Connaught to become an established Heritage Town. As well as visiting the medieval heritage centre, children can dress up in authentic medieval costume, play medieval games such as skittles and also have a go at traditional archery or play in the medieval maze.

Athenry Castle

Athenry, Co Galway
Tel: 091-844797   Fax: 091-845796
athenrycastle@opw.ie   www.heritageireland.ie

- Open daily, June to mid-September, 10.00 to 6.00; mid-September to October and April to May, 10.00 to 5.00
- Adults, €2.90; Children, €1.30; Family, €7.40
- Located in heritage town of Athenry

Athenry is one of the most notable medieval walled towns surviving in Ireland, owing its foundation to Meiler de Bermingham who built his Castle there c.1250. The great three-storey tower, surrounded by defensive walls, is entered at first-floor level through an unusual decorated doorway. Recently re-roofed, the interior contains an audio-visual room and exhibition. Access to ground floor of Castle for people with disabilities. *An OPW site.*

Aughnanure Castle
Oughterard, Co Galway
Tel: 091-552214   Fax: 091-557244
www.heritageireland.ie

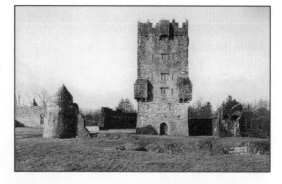

- Open daily mid-June to September, 9.30 to 6.00; open weekends, May to mid-June, October, 9.30 to 6.00
- Adults, €2.90; Children, €1.30; Family, €7.40
- Located 3.5 km from Oughterard off N59

Built by the O'Flahertys c. 1500, Aughnanure Castle lies in picturesque surroundings close to the shores of Lough Corrib. Standing on what is virtually a rocky island, the Castle is a particularly well-preserved example of an Irish tower house. In addition, visitors will find the remains of a banqueting hall, a watch tower, an unusual double bawn and bastions and a dry harbour. Access to Castle grounds is restricted for wheelchair users. *An OPW site.*

Battle of Aughrim Visitor Centre
Aughrim, Ballinasloe, Co Galway
Tel: 0905-73939

- Open June 1 to September 8, Tuesday to Saturday, 10.00 to 6.00; Sunday, 2.00 to 6.00
- Adults, €4.00; Children, €2.90, Family, €8.05
- Located in Aughrim village on the Dublin-Galway road
- Caters for school groups/tours
- Children's worksheets available

The Battle of Aughrim — heard by the citizens of Galway over 35 miles away — was the final battle of the War of the Two Kings, Kings James III and William of Orange, and sealed the fate of the Jacobite army. On 12 July, 1691, 45,000 soldiers from nine European nations fought and 9,000 perished on the Aughrim slopes. Today, visitors can discover the original Twelfth of July and the roots of Ireland's turbulent history at this award-winning centre.

Brigit's Garden

Pollagh, Roscahill, Co Galway
Tel: 091-550905   Fax: 091-550491
info@galwaygarden.com   www.galwaygarden.com

- Open from mid-April to end of September, 9.30 to 5.30
- Adults, €6.75; Children, €4.00; Family, €20.00, under-fives free of charge
- Located on the N59, between Moycullen and Oughterard, 20 minutes from Galway
- Caters for school groups/tours
- Caters for children's parties
- Has special programmes for children

Brigit's Garden sits in 11 acres of gardens, woodlands and meadows. It consists of four unique gardens representing the old Celtic festivals and featuring basket swings, a throne and a giant earth woman. There is a kids' discovery trail, a stone chamber, a ring-fort and a living willow play area. School visits are available year round and a programme of special events for children is available in the summer.

Connemara National Park

Letterfrack, Co Galway
Tel: 095-41054   Fax: 095-41005
www.heritageireland.ie

- Open daily mid-March to May, 10.00 to 5.30; June, 10.00 to 6.30; July to August, 9.30 to 6.30; September to mid-October, 10.00 to 5.30
- Adults, €2.90; Children, €1.30; Family, €7.40
- Located in Letterfrack village

Connemara National Park covers some 2,000 hectares (4,942 acres) of scenic countryside, rich in wildlife on the slopes of the Twelve Bens. Attractions include exhibitions, nature trails and an audio-visual show, "Man and the Landscape". In addition there is a summer programme of walks, talks and special events for younger visitors. Access for visitors with disabilities in the Visitor Centre. *An OPW site.*

Coole Park and Gardens

Gort, Co Galway
Tel: 091-631804
info@coolepark.ie   www.coolepark.ie

- Open daily June to August, 10.00 to 6.00; September, 10.00 to 5.00; open Tuesday to Sunday, April to May, 10.00 to 5.00
- Adults, €2.90; Children, €1.30; Family, €7.40
- Located 3 km north of Gort on N18

Coole Park, now a nature reserve, was the home of Lady Augusta Gregory, dramatist and co-founder with Edward Martyn and W.B. Yeats of the Abbey Theatre. Attractions include exhibitions, tea-rooms, nature trail walks, the famous "Autograph Tree", and a lake and turlough. There are two audio-visual presentations, "The Magic of Coole" and "Lady Gregory of Coole". *An OPW site.*

Corrib Cruises

Oughterard, Co Galway and Cong, Co Mayo
Tel: 094-9546029   Fax: 094-9546568
info@corribcruises.com   www.corribcruises.com

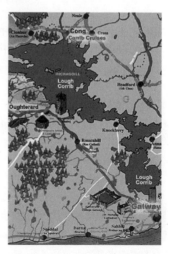

- Open in Oughterard, April to October; open in Cong year round
- Cost: €15.00 per person; Family ticket, €35.00
- Located at Oughterard Pier in Oughterard, and Lisloughry Pier in Cong
- Caters for school groups/tours

Corrib Cruises offers pleasure cruises on Lough Corrib, Ireland's largest lake and one of the most scenic in Europe. All trips are from 1 hour to 90 minutes and include a 20-minute guided tour of Inchagoil Island. Also included are panoramic views of Ashford Castle, guided commentary on islands, lake and shoreline, a spacious sundeck and comfortable indoor seating.

Dan O'Hara's Heritage and History Centre

Lettershea, Clifden, Co. Galway
Tel: 095-21808 / 21246   Fax: 095-22098
danohara@eircom.net   www.connemaraheritage.com

eritageISLAND
IRELAND'S VISITOR ATTRACTIONS

- Open April to October, 10.00 to 6.00
- Adults, €7.50; Children, €4.00; Family, €18.00
- Located on the main Galway to Clifden road, 6 km from Clifden
- Caters for school groups/tours

Award-winning Dan O'Hara's Heritage and History Centre, listed as one of Ireland's top tourist attractions, offers a unique experience which should be part of everyone's visit to the West. Start with an audio-visual presentation in various languages, view the History Room exhibits, visit the Crannóg (showing how Celts used to live), Ringfort, Oratory, thatched cottage with open peat fire, animals including famous Connemara ponies and archaeological site, or plant a tree in memory of your ancestors

Dartfield — Ireland's Horseworld Museum and Park

Kilreekill, Loughrea, Co Galway
Tel: 091-843968   Fax: 091-843969
info@dartfieldhorsemuseum.com
www.dartfieldhorsemuseum.com

eritageISLAND
IRELAND'S VISITOR ATTRACTIONS

- Open daily year round, 9.30 to 6.00
- Adults, €7.00; Children/OAP, €4.50; Family, €16.00
- Located on the main Galway to Dublin road (N6)
- Caters for school groups/tours

Horseworld at Dartfield, a unique horse museum and park, is truly a wonderful interpretation of the horse, emphasising the relationship between the Irish and their horses. Lots of interesting displays including a gallery, forge, saddlery, carriages, hall of fame, library and lots more. Horse-riding lessons and trail riding are also available.

Dún Aonghasa

Kilmurvey, Inishmore, Aran Islands, Co Galway
Tel: 099-61008   Fax: 099-61009
www.heritageireland.ie

- Open daily April to October, 10.00 to 6.00; November to March, 10.00 to 4.00
- Adults, €2.10; Children, €1.30; Family, €5.80
- Located 7 km west of Kilronan (local boat service from Galway and Rossaville)

Perched spectacularly on a cliff overlooking the Atlantic Ocean, this is the largest of the prehistoric stone forts of the Aran Islands. It is enclosed by three massive dry-stone walls and a "chevaux-de-frise" consisting of tall blocks of limestone set vertically into the ground to deter attackers. The fort is about 900 metres from the Visitor Centre and is approached over rising ground. Access for visitors with disabilities to the Visitor Centre. *An OPW site.*

Dunguaire Castle

Kinvara, Co Galway
Tel: 061 360788   Fax: 061-361020
reservations@shannondev.ie   www.shannonheritage.com

- Open daily May 1 to October 30, 9.30 to 5.00
- Adults, €4.75; Children, €2.95; Family, €12.50
- Located in Kinvara, Co Galway
- Caters for school groups/tours

Dunguaire Castle has, for hundreds of years, stood proudly on the site of the seventh-century stronghold of Guaire, the King of Connaught. The Castle bridges 13 centuries of Irish history, from the skirmishes, battles and sieges that characterise its colourful past, through to the literary revival of the twentieth century. In 1924, Oliver St. John Gogarty, surgeon, poet, author and wit, a contemporary and friend of W.B. Yeats and Lady Gregory, acquired the Castle as a place of quiet retreat.

Errislannan Manor Gardens

Errislannan Manor, Clifden, Co Galway
Tel: 095-21133   Fax: 095-21670
www.errislannanmanor.com

- Open April to October,
  9.00 to 6.00
- Admission: €5.00 per person
- Located 4 miles south of Clifden on the
  Ballyconneely road (L102)

The Garden is open to the public under the
Royal Horticultural Society of Ireland
Gardens for Charity scheme. The garden is
kept going by Stephanie Brooks in loving memory of her late husband, Donal Meredith Brooks, who
devoted much of his retirement to it continuous upkeep and expansion. There is also a children's
playground and pony riding.

Galway Atlantaquaria

National Aquarium of Ireland, Salthill, Galway
Tel: 091-585100   Fax: 091-584360
atlantaquaria@eircom.net   www.nationalaquarium.com

HeritageISLAND
IRELAND'S VISITOR ATTRACTIONS

- Open daily April to September, 9.00 to 6.00;
  October to March, Wednesday to Sunday,
  10.00 to 5.00
- Adults, €8.00; Children, €5.00; Family,
  €24.00
- Located on the Promenade in Salthill
- Caters for children's parties
- Caters for school groups/tours
- Special programmes for children

Galway Atlantaquaria is Ireland's National Aquarium and is home to 170 species of fresh water and
marine life. Designed over two floors, visitors follow a vivid interpretation of the Irish aquatic
landscape: from the glacial mountain streams of Connemara, down through the famous River Corrib and out
into Galway Bay. On the journey exhibits include salmon, seahorses, octopus, stingrays and a real 60ft
whale skeleton. The aquarium also boasts four types of native Irish shark including the rare angel shark and
venomous spurdog. Visitors can take part in the feeding, explore the model submarine, and even hold
starfish and giant spider crabs.

Kiltartan Gregory Museum and Millennium Park

Kiltartan Cross, Gort, Co Galway
Tel: 091-631069   Fax: 091-631482
www.gortonline.com/gregorymuseum

- Open daily June to September, 10.00 to 6.00; October to May, open Sundays, 1.00 to 5.00
- Contact museum for admission costs
- Located 2 miles NE of Gort on N18
- Caters for school groups/tours

Kiltartan Gregory Museum is housed in an old schoolhouse and one room has been retained as an old Irish classroom as it was 100 years ago. The larger room contains material relating to WB Yeats, Lady Gregory – who immortalised Kiltartan in her books and plays – and the Gaelic Revival. There is also considerable emphasis placed on local history. Nearby is the Kiltartan Millennium Park and picnic area.

Kylemore Abbey and Garden

Connemara, Co Galway
Tel: 095-41146   Fax: 095-41440
info@kylemoreabbey.ie   www.kylemoreabbey.com

Heritage ISLAND
IRELAND'S VISITOR ATTRACTIONS

- Open March to November, 9.30 to 5.30; November to March, 10.30-4.00
- Adults, €11.00, OAP, €7.00
- Located 50 miles from Galway on N59
- Caters for school groups/tours

Set in the heart of the Connemara mountains is the Kylemore Abbey Estate, home of the Irish Benedictine Nuns. Visitors can see the picturesque Abbey (reception rooms, video and exhibition), and enjoy a stroll to the beautifully restored Gothic Church (under restoration). Kylemore Abbey's six-acre Victorian Walled Garden is the most significant walled garden in the west. A visit to the west of Ireland is not complete without experiencing the beauty and tranquillity that is Kylemore Abbey and Garden.

Leenane Cultural Centre

Leenane, Co Galway
Tel: 095-42323   Fax: 095-42337
noeot@eircom.net   www.leenane-connemara.com

- Open daily April to October, 9.00 to 6.00 (other times by appointment)
- Adults, €3.00; Children, €2.00; Family, €7.00
- Located in Leenane village
- Caters for school groups/tours

A beautiful purpose-built visitor centre, the Leenane Cultural Centre is wheelchair accessible throughout. Interpretative centre based on local sheep industry and wool handcrafts. Demonstrations of carding, spinning and weaving with information on plant dyes. The history of sheep is shown as various live breeds of sheep can be viewed in a beautiful setting overlooking Killary Harbour. Local history and places of interest are highlighted in a continuous audio-visual display in English, Irish, German, French and Italian.

Leisure World Galway

Galway Shopping Centre, Headford Road, Galway
Tel: 091-562820   Fax: 091-564331
info@leisureworld.ie   www.leisureworld.ie

- Open May to September, 10.00 to midnight; October to April, 1.00 to midnight
- No entrance fee; costs vary for individual activities
- Located in Galway city centre
- Caters for school groups/tours
- Caters for children's parties

Leisure World is an all-weather family recreation centre which includes Ten-Pin Bowling, Kiddies Adventureland, Pool/Snooker Tables, Air Hockey Tables and the latest Video Pursuits. Cosmic Bumper Bowling includes a computerised scoring system, bowling bumpers and lighter balls to ensure that even the youngest children enjoy their bowling experience. Leisure World is a very popular birthday party location with seven party packages to suit children of all ages.

Portumna Castle

Portumna, Co Galway
Tel: 090-9741658   Fax: 090-9741889
portumnacastle@ealga.ie   www.heritageireland.ie

- Open from April 1 to October 31
- Adults, €2.10; Children. €1.30; Family, €5.80
- Located in Portumna Town and Forest Park
- Caters for school groups/tours (free admission)
- Special programmes for children

Portumna Castle, built in 1618 and badly damaged by fire in 1826, is now a semi-ruin with restored gardens surrounding it. A free guided tour is given to all on request bringing the castle to life with history and stories. A quiz is also provided for school tours on request. Surrounding the castle grounds are 1,000 acres of woodland with colour co-ordinated walking trails. To the north of the castle is a well-equipped playground and there is also a picnic area in the forest park. *An OPW site.*

Rathbaun Farm

Ardrahan, Co Galway
Tel/Fax: 091-635385
info@rathbaunfarm.com   www.rathbaunfarm.com

HeritageISLAND
IRELAND'S VISITOR ATTRACTIONS

- Open daily March to October, 9.00 to 5.30;
- Fees: Visit only, €5.00; morning coffee/afternoon tea and visit, €9.00; lunch and visit, €17.00; group rates available
- Located in Ardrahan Village, 30km from Galway

Visitors to Rathbaun Farm will be enchanted by its thatched cottage home, turf fire, stone walls and an array of animals. Time spent here gives a glimpse into the daily workings of a sheep-farm with plenty of time to see the animals, feed the lambs, talk to the family and explore the farmyard.

Teach an Phiarsaigh (Patrick Pearse's Cottage)

Ros Muc, Galway
Tel: 091-574292
tanphiarsaigh@opw.ie   www.heritageireland.ie

- Open daily mid-June to September, 10.00 to 6.00; open weekends Easter to mid-June, 10.00 to 5.00
- Adults, €1.60; Children, €1.10; Family, €4.50
- Located off R340

👨 👨

Patrick Pearse, the executed leader of the 1916 Rising, spent some of his leisure time in this modest thatched cottage where he took the opportunity to improve his knowledge of the Irish language among the local speakers. The interior, although burned during the War of Independence, has been reconstructed and contains a number of mementoes of Pearse, the idealistic school teacher, whose rebellion and death are considered to have been a turning point in Irish history. *An OPW site.*

Thoor Ballylee

Gort, Co Galway
Tel: 091-631436 (091-537700 October to May)
thoorballylee@irelandwest.ie

- Open June to September, Monday to Saturday, 9.30 to 5.00
- Adults, €6.00; Students, €5.50; Family, €12.00
- Located 1 km off N18 Galway—Limerick road
- Caters for school groups/tours

♿ 👨 👨 🎁

Thoor Ballylee is well known as the summer home of the poet W.B. Yeats and as the setting of his poems "The Winding Stair" and "The Tower". The tower was originally a Norman fortified house owned by the powerful de Burgo family during the thirteenth and fourteenth centuries. Yeats bought the castle in 1916 for £35.00. Today visitors can see an audio-visual presentation of the history of Yeats' life and the tower and hear push-button audio narrations in each room of the tower.

Turoe Pet Farm and Leisure Park

Turoe House, Bullaun, Loughrea, Co Galway
Tel: 091-841580   Fax: 091-841580
turoefarm@esatclear.ie   www.turoepetfarm.com

- Open daily Easter to September, 10.00 to 7.00; October to Easter, 1.00 to 6.00 weekends only.
- Adults, €6.00; Children, €10.00
- Located 6 km north of Loughrea off R350
- Caters for children's parties
- Caters for school groups/tours
- Special programmes for children

Located in a beautiful rural setting, the 14-acre Turoe Pet Farm and Leisure Park has extensive all-weather facilities including a nature trail, outdoor playgrounds, indoor play area with Adventure Land and bouncing castles, pets corner, indoor picnic area, pool room and more. Special events for children at Easter, Hallowe'en, Christmas and throughout the year.

The Cavan and Leitrim Railway

Station Road, Dromod, Co Leitrim
Tel: 071-9638599
info@irish-railway.com   www.irish-railway.com

- Open daily January 2 to December 23, 10.00 to. 5.00; Sunday, 1.00 to 5.00
- Children, €5.00; Family, €16.00
- Located in Dromod village next to Iarnrod Eireann station

At Cavan and Leitrim Railway visitors can step back in time and travel on a narrow gauge train, visit the transport museum, sit in the cockpit of an old plane, or imagine they are a soldier in an armoured car. There are trains, buses, fire tenders, guns and planes on display. At Hallowe'en there is the scariest Ghost Train in Ireland!

Parke's Castle

Fivemilebourne, Co Leitrim
Tel: 071-9164149
www.heritageireland.ie

- Open daily mid-March to October, 10.00 to 6.00
- Adults, €2.90; Children, €1.30; Family, €7.40
- Located 11 km from Sligo Town on R286

🍽 ♿ ♟

A restored plantation castle of the early seventeenth century, picturesquely situated on the shores of Lough Gill, once the home of Robert Parke and his family. The Courtyard grounds contain evidence of an earlier sixteenth century Tower House structure once owned by Sir Brian O'Rourke who subsequently was executed at Tyburn, London in 1591. The Castle has been restored using Irish oak and traditional craftsmanship. Access for visitors with disabilities to ground floor. *An OPW site.*

Céide Fields Visitor Centre

Céide Fields, Ballycastle, Co Mayo
Tel: 096-43325   Fax: 096-43261
ceidefields@opw.ie   www.heritageireland.ie

- Open mid-March to end of November, 10.00 to 5.00 (June to September until 6.00)
- Adults, €3.70; Children, €1.30; Family, €8.70
- Located 5 miles west of Ballycastle on R314
- Caters for school groups/tours

🍽   ♟

The Céide Fields are the remains of a Stone Age farmed landscape preserved for over 5,000 years beneath a blanket of peat. The award-winning pyramid-shaped visitor centre is spectacularly located beside the north Mayo cliffs, with a viewing platform that allows visitors to look down safely to the sea 365 feet below. Guided tours of the site explain how the landscape changed from forest to farmland to bogland, and tell the story of the everyday lives of our Neolithic ancestors. Exhibitions include life-size models of a Neolithic family, including the children's favourite — the "granny" in bed. *An OPW site.*

Mayo Leisure Point

Moneen, Castlebar, Co Mayo
Tel: 094-9025473
www.mayoleisurepoint.ie

- Open daily year round, 10.00 to midnight
- Costs vary depending on activity
- Located in village of Moneen
- Caters for children's parties
- Caters for school groups/tours

Mayo Leisure Point, with 70,000-square feet, is Ireland's largest indoor entertainment park. Activities include Mayo Roller Bowl, Northwest Karting (for children 8+), Castle Leisure Club, Mayo Movie World, and Kachina Natural Spa. Special features for children include Nokey's Adventureland, Lazer 0-2000 and video games.

National Museum of Country Life

Turlough Park, Castlebar, Co Mayo
Tel: 094-9031755   Fax: 094-9031583
tpark@museum.ie   www.museum.ie

- Open year round, Tuesday to Saturday, 10.00 to 5.00; Sunday, 2.00 to 5.00
- No entrance fee
- Located 4 miles from Castlebar off the N5 in Turlough Village
- Caters for school groups/tours

Home to the national folklife collection, the Museum of Country Life is the first branch of the National Museum to be located outside of Dublin. Visitors to the Museum will see a vanished world of Irish country life between 1850 and 1950, made real again through the vivid detail of domestic furniture and utensils, hunting, fishing and agricultural implements, objects relating to games and pastimes, religion and education, dress and footwear. A Summer School for children is held in July.

Westport Heritage Town

Clew Bay Heritage Centre, The Quay, Westport, Co Mayo
Tel/Fax: 098-26852
westportheritage@eircom.net   www.museumsofmayo.com   ⊞eritageISLAND
                                                          IRELAND'S VISITOR ATTRACTIONS

- Open June to September, Monday to Friday,
  10.00 to 5.00; Sunday, 3.00 to 5.00;
  October, April, May, Monday to Friday,
  10.00 to 2.00
- Adults, €3.00; Students, €2.00; Children,
  free (accompanied by an adult)
- Located in Westport on the Quay
- Caters for school groups/tours

Westport is situated on the shores of Clew
Bay, in the shadow of Croagh Patrick and is one of the few planned towns in the country. It is an estate town, built to the plan of James Wyatt, the well-known architect of the Georgian period. One of its outstanding features is the elegant tree-lined boulevard, known as The Mall. The history of the development of Westport, from the time it was an O'Malley stronghold in the sixteenth century, to the present day, is brought alive in the Clew Bay Heritage Centre, located at Westport Quay.

Westport House and Country Park

Westport, Co Mayo
Tel: 098-27766   Fax: 098-25206
info@westporthouse,ie   www.westporthouse.ie   ⊞eritageISLAND
                                                   IRELAND'S VISITOR ATTRACTIONS

- Open March to September; October/November
  (weekends only); check website for details
- Family day ticket available (contact for details)
- Located in Westport near the harbour
- Caters for children's parties
- Caters for school groups/tours
- Special facilities for children

Westport House Country Park, located in a
magnificent setting, is one of the most popular family destinations in Ireland with over 4,000,000 visitors welcomed. Attractions for children include the Children's Animal and Bird Park, Log Flume Ride, Jungle World (4'7" height restriction), boating on lake, pitch & putt, Hill Slide (eight years and over), Slippery Dip, Swan Pedaloes (accompanied by an adult only), Miniature Train Ride, Model Railway, children's playground and much more.

Arigna Mining Experience

Derreenavoggy, Arigna, Co Roscommon
Tel: 071-9646466
www.arignaminingexperience.ie

- Open all year, 10.00 to 5.00
- Adults, €8.00; Children, €6.00; Family rates available
- Located on the R280 outside of Carrick-on-Shannon
- Caters for school groups/tours

Visitors to the Arigna Mining Experience can discover and experience the life of a coal miner through a unique underground tour of what was Ireland's last working coal mine. With an ex-miner as a guide, visitors will learn about the history, geology, human endurance and indeed the incredible life stories of the miners who worked there.

Boyle Abbey

Boyle, Co Roscommon
Tel: 071-9662604
www.heritageireland.ie

- Open April to October, 10.00 to 6.00
- Adults, €2.10; Children, €1.30; Family, €5.80
- Located in Boyle town off the N4

An impressive and well-preserved Cistercian Monastery which was founded in the twelfth century under the patronage of the local ruling family, the MacDermotts. Though mutilated during the seventeenth and eighteenth centuries when it was used to accommodate a military garrison, Boyle Abbey nevertheless retains its ability to impress the visitor as one of the most formidable of the early Cistercian foundations in Ireland. A restored gatehouse of sixteenth/seventeenth century houses an exhibition. Restricted access for people with disabilities. *An OPW site.*

Encountering Heritage

Beatrice Kelly

The idea of introducing children to heritage can be daunting as visions of trailing around dusty museums comes to mind or walking through driving rain to see an amorphous heap of earth in a soggy field. However, these images need not be the reality as the diversity of heritage means that a variety of activities offers the chance to encounter aspects of it in an enjoyable and entertaining way. The National Museums in Dublin and Castlebar (Country Life) and Dúchas the Heritage Service offer a range of activities geared to children at sites around the country and it is well worth contacting them to find out what is available. On a more low-key note, a trip to the beach, cycling through a park or forest, or walking up a mountain could also encourage an interest in some area of heritage.

Opportunities are also present in primary schools. Since 1999 the Heritage Council and the INTO have been running the Heritage in Schools Scheme whereby a heritage practitioner visits a primary school for either a day or a half-day. The visit is part-funded by the school and the remainder of the expenses are covered by the Heritage Council.

The project has a number of aims:

1. To generate greater awareness, interest and appreciation of our heritage among the younger generation — this also spreads on to the parents.

2. To encourage teachers and pupils to leave the classroom and enjoy their local heritage at first hand.

3. Schools will establish relations with heritage specialists and the Heritage Council — many schools ask the same specialist back at different stages of the year. This can be particularly beneficial for seasonal activities.

4. Heritage matters will have a real and vibrant role in our primary schools — we want the visit of the heritage specialist to be integrated into the school plan, not seen as a variation of the summer school trip.

A panel of 84 people is available nationwide covering a range of activities from birdwatching, bread-making, archaeological excavation and wood crafts. Each heritage specialist brings their excitement and enthusiasm for their subject into the classroom, and where possible, will lead people from the classroom to the great outdoors.

The panel offers a varied team reflecting the complexity of Ireland's heritage and there are many ways in which schools can avail of this expertise. Here are a number of suggestions from Leo Hallissey, Letterfrack NS, who was the main instigator of the idea and who has made use of the excitement available through this scheme:

- Plan a year's programme and allow for a couple of heritage slots per term. Remember seasonality plays a part if you want to do field work.

- Plan a number of visits around one specialist. This method gives a great sense of continuity and the children really get to know their visitor.

- Other people bring two or more specialists to the school and make an event of the visit — like the cross-pollination that occurs when a botanist and an archaeologist visit the school.

- Some people prefer to plan a "Heritage Week" per term and invite a team of at least three disciplines for each week. Parents and the community at large could be involved in an event like this and it offers the chance to put up exhibitions and displays.

- Use could also be made of the Writers in Schools Scheme as it is lovely to combine an archaeologist with a visit from someone like Marita Conlon McKenna whose novels sometimes have a historic background or an ecologist like Gordon D'Arcy with a nature writer like Tom McCaughren.

All primary schools have received the updated directory of heritage specialists. Information is also available on the INTO web site — www.INTO.ie — and directly from Linda Johnston in the INTO.

Beatrice Kelly is the Inland Waterways and Marine and Coastal Officer at the Heritage Council in Kilkenny.

Claypipe Visitors Centre

Knockcroghery Village, Co Roscommon
Tel: 090-6661923
ethelkelly@eircom.net

- Open May to September, Monday to Friday, 10.00 to 6.00
- No entrance fee
- Located in Knockcroghery Village, between Athlone and Roscommon on the N61

The village of Knockcroghery was famous for almost 300 years as a centre for the production of clay pipes or "dudeens". They were particularly popular at wakes, where trays of tobacco-filled pipes, Guinness and whiskey would be laid out for mourners. Production of the pipes ceased abruptly on June 19, 1921 when the Black and Tans burned down the village. The craft of clay pipe manufacture has now been revived and visitors can watch pipes being made using the original tools and methods.

Cruachan Aí Visitor Centre

Tulsk, Co Roscommon
Tel: 071-9639268
cruachanai@esatclear.ie   www.cruachanai.com

HeritageISLAND
IRELAND'S VISITOR ATTRACTIONS

- Open Monday to Saturday, June to September, 9.00 to 6.00, Sunday, 1.00 to 5.00;; October to May, Monday to Saturday, 9.00 to 5.00
- Adults, €5.00; Family, €12.00
- Located in Tulsk village at junction of N5 and N61
- Caters for school groups/tours

🍴 ♿ 🚻 🎁

In the heartland of Connaught, a forgotten landscape is being brought to light in the award-winning Cruachan Aí Visitor Centre. Cruachan is one of the best preserved Celtic Royal Sites in Europe located in the medieval village of Tulsk, Co Roscommon. An amazing array of archaeological remains are located within a four-mile radius of the centre, dating from the Stone Age to the historic period, and these are interpreted in bright, modern exhibition rooms, using the latest DVD technology. The legendary Cruachan was a Royal Palace, home of Medb (or Maeve), Warrior Queen and Earth Goddess. Fierce and proud, she was responsible for launching the famed cattle raid of Cooley, as recounted in one of the greatest works of early Irish literature, the *Táin Bó Cuailnge*.

Derryglad Folk Museum

Curraghboy, Athlone, Co Roscommon
Tel: 090-6488192   Fax: 090-6488192

- Open May to September, Monday to Saturday, 10.00 to 6.00; Sunday, 2.00 to 6.00
- Adults, €5.00; Children, €3.50; Family, €15.00
- Located on Curraghboy Road off the Tuam Road outside Athlone
- Caters for children's parties
- Caters for school groups/tours
- Special programmes for children

Derryglad Folk Museum is privately owned and houses a unique 25-year collection of horse-drawn machinery restored to original working order, tradesmen's tools, buttermaking equipment, thatched bar and grocery, old and rare washing machines, collection of sheep shears and a wide-ranging collection of indoor and outdoor rural artefacts.

King House Interpretive Galleries and Museum

Main Street, Boyle, Co Roscommon
Tel: 071-9663242   Fax: 071-9663243
kinghouse@roscommoncoco.ie   www.kinghouse.ie

Heritage**ISLAND**
IRELAND'S VISITOR ATTRACTIONS

- Open daily April to September, 10.00 to 6.00
- Adults, €7.00; Children, €4.00; Family, €18.00
- Located in town centre
- Caters for school groups/tours

King House is a magnificently restored Georgian Mansion built around 1730 by Sir Henry King. Today, with the aid of exciting special effects and life-size models in recreated scenes, visitors to King House are taken back through its long and impressive history in an entertaining and informative manner. Children can write like the monks of Boyle Abbey with a quill and ink, or even dress in the attire of a Gaelic Chieftain. Test building skills in constructing a brick vault and play the regimental drum of the Connaught Rangers. Children will also love the adventure playground adjacent to King House.

Lough Key Forest Park

Rockingham, Boyle, Co Roscommon
Tel: 071-9662363
seamusduignan@coillte.ie
www.coillte.ie/tourism_and_recreation

- Open daily April to October, 10.00 to 6.00
- Entrance fee: Car, €5.00; Coach, €20.00
- Located 7 miles west of Carrick-on-Shannon
- Caters for school groups/tours

♿ 👫

Located in a scenic and historical area of Roscommon, Lough Key consists of approximately 350 hectares of forested areas and open parkland. Some of the features include tunnels, a viewing tower, ice-house, bog garden and gazebo. Approximately 10 km of forest walks take visitors through magnificent lake shore, canal banks and trees. The park offers a haven of tranquillity in peaceful surroundings in an area of great natural beauty.

Strokestown Park House and Gardens

Strokestown, Co Roscommon
Tel: 071-9633013   Fax: 071-9633712
info@strokestownpark.ie   www.strokestownpark.ie

- Open daily from mid-March to end October, 11.00 to 5.30
- Entrance fees available on request
- Located on the N5, 23 km from Longford
- Caters for school groups/tours

🍴 ♿ 👫 🎁

Strokestown Park House and Gardens includes three separate attractions. The House is an eighteenth-century mansion which has been faithfully restored. It is unique in that it retains its original furnishings and professionally guided tours allow visitors to browse freely through the stately surroundings. The four-acre eighteenth-century walled pleasure garden has been fully restored to its original splendour. The Famine Museum uses a combination of original documents and images from the Strokestown Park collection to explain the circumstances of the Great Irish Famine of the 1840s. This collection boasts an extensive range of papers including actual letters written by the tenants on the Strokestown Estate at the time of the Famine.

Carrowmore Megalithic Cemetery

Sligo Town
Tel: 071-9161534
carrowmoretomb@opw.ie   www.heritageireland.ie

- Open daily April to October, 10.00 to 6.00
- Adults, €2.10; Children, €1.10; Family, €5.80
- Located 4 km from Sligo town centre off the R252

This is the largest cemetery of megalithic tombs in Ireland and is also among the country's oldest. Over 60 tombs have been located by archaeologists; the oldest pre-date Newgrange by some 700 years. A restored cottage houses a small exhibition relating to the site. Restricted access in centre for people with disabilities (tombs are inaccessible to people with disabilities). *An OPW site.*

Eagles Flying/Irish Raptor Research Centre

Ballymote, Co Sligo
Tel: 071-9189310   Fax: 071-9189310
eaglesflying@utvinternet.com1   www.eaglesflying.com

- Open daily 10.30 to 12.30 and 2.30 to 4.30 from April 1 to November 7
- Adults, €8.00; Children, €5.00; Family and group rates available
- Located on the N17 between Ballymote and Ballinacarrow

At Eagles Flying, Ireland's biggest sanctuary for birds of prey and owls, visitors can watch eagles, hawks, falcons and owls fly right over their heads. Some of the birds can even be touched. During the show scientists inform visitors about these magnificent creatures and answer any questions. There are also birds in aviaries to look at and a pet zoo with rabbits, guinea pigs, goats, lambs, ferrets, donkeys and many more to pet.

Knocknashee — Legendary Hill of the Faeries

Lavagh, Near Tubbercurry, Co Sligo
Tel: 071-9130286   Fax: 071-9130286
gillighans@eircom.net   www.gillighansworld.com

- Open 11.00 to 7.00; Friday, Saturday and Sunday from May 1 to September 7; rest of season, open Tuesday to Sunday; open December 5 to 12 for Santa and Winter Wonderland. Closed first weekend of September.
- Adults, €7.00; Children, €6.00; Family and group rates available
- Located off the Sligo—Tubbercurry Road (N17)

At Knocknashee, visitors can escape into a land of artistry and imagination, a magical place adored by both children and adults. Miniature villages and delightful faerie habitats nestle in beautiful water and botanic gardens with a stone tunnel entrance, dolmens and amphitheatre. Enchanted glade, secluded picnic areas, pet village, water cave and spectacular views from Fort Faerie. It's been called "a little piece of heaven on earth, a unique experience, a real Irish fairyland".

Lissadell House and Gardens

Ballinfull, Sligo
Tel: 071-9163150
info@lissadellhouse.com   www.lissadellhouse.com

- Open daily from March 16 to September 30
- Adults, €6.00; Children, €3.00
- Located north of Sligo Town on the N4
- Caters for school groups/tours

Lissadell House was the childhood home of patriot Constance Markievicz and inspiration of poet W.B. Yeats. One hundred years ago it was also the premier horticultural estate in Ireland. This horticultural enterprise was created by Josslyn Gore Booth, brother to Constance. Today Lissadell House and Gardens are undergoing major restoration and children can see this exciting work in progress.

Model Arts and Niland Gallery

The Mall, Sligo
Tel: 071-9141405
info@modelart.ie   www.modelart.ie

- Open Tuesday to Sunday, 10.00 to 5.30
- No entrance fee
- Located on the Mall in Sligo Town
- Special programmes for children

The Model Arts and Niland Gallery is a vibrant centre for the arts in Sligo, hosting work from all over the world. Built in 1842 as a Model School, the present building was completely refurbished, extended and reopened to wide acclaim in 2001. One of the premier gallery spaces in Ireland, the Model Arts and Niland Gallery is complemented by an intimate performance space, with regular music, recitals, readings and films. There are numerous programmes, workshops, classes and special events for children and young people throughout the year.

Sligo Abbey

Abbey Street, Sligo
Tel: 071-9146406
sligoabbey@opw.ie   www.heritageireland.ie

- Open daily April to October, 10.00 to 6.00
- Adults, €2.10; Children, €1.10; Family, €5.80
- Located in centre of Sligo

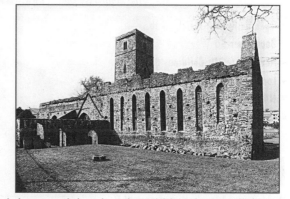

Known locally as the Abbey, this Dominican Friary was founded in the mid-thirteenth century by Maurice FitzGerald. The site contains a great wealth of carvings including Gothic and Renaissance tomb sculpture, well preserved cloisters and the only sculptured fifteenth century high altar to survive in any Irish monastic church. This enigmatic Friary will inspire and enlighten its visitors. Access to site is by stone stairway. *An OPW site.*

Sligo Folk Park

Riverstown, Co Sligo
Tel: 071-9165001
sligofolkpark@eircom.net   wwwsligofolkpark.com

- Open mid-April to October, Monday to Saturday, 10.00 to 5.30; Sunday, 12.30 to 6.00. November to April, open by appointment
- Adults, €5.00; Children, €3.00;
- Located just off the N4 in east Co Sligo
- Caters for school groups/tours
- Special programmes for children

ﺗ⦿⦿   ♿   ♂♀   🎁

At Sligo Folk Park visitors can experience rural Irish heritage and culture from times gone by deep in the heart of Sligo. Included within the Park is a traditional cottage named Mrs Buckley's Cottage, as well as Millview House which originates from the late nineteenth century and is surrounded by open workshops in which historical artefacts are restored to their former glory. Other attractions include a fully equipped forge, a replicated classroom, a complete range of restored agricultural implements, plus geese, turkeys, peacocks, rabbits, goats, hens and ducks.

Waterpoint

Pier Road, Enniscrone, Co Sligo
Tel: 096-36999   Fax: 096-36988
info@waterpoint.ie   www.waterpoint.ie

- Open weekends, 11.00 to 8.00; Pool open weekdays, 4.00 to 10.00; Gym open weekdays, 10.00 to 10.00
- Adults, €7.00; Children, €4.50; Infants, €3.00
- Located on Pier Road in Enniscrone
- Caters for children's parties
- Caters for school groups/tours
- Special programmes for children

ﺗ⦿⦿   ♿   ♂♀   🎁

Facilities at Waterpoint include a children's fun pool, a 65-metre water slide, 16.5 metre pool, a fitness gym with an activity hall, steam room, jacuzzi and sauna.

Wild Rose Tour Boat

Kilmore, Fivemilebourne, Co Sligo
Tel: 071-9164266   Fax: 071-9164266

- Open from Easter to October, 9.30 to 6.30
- Cost: €6.00 per child; families and groups negotiable
- Located in Sligo Town and Parkes Castle, Co Leitrim
- Caters for children's parties
- Caters for school groups/tours

The Wild Rose Waterbus operates on one of the most beautiful and scenic lakes in Ireland, Lough Gill. This majestic all-weather craft travels between historic Parkes Castle on the shores of Lough Gill into the centre of Sligo town. En route the Wild Rose takes in the famous "Isle of Innisfree". During the trip the skipper, George McGoldrick, will recite tales of folklore, history and poetry associated with Ireland's most famous son, W.B. Yeats. A worksheet is provided for children and prizes given at the end of the trip. Some children may even get to steer the boat!

Planning a Great Day Out?

For information on over 90 of Ireland's leading Visitor
Attractions and Heritage Towns, fun visits for all the family and news
of what's on there really is only one choice:

WWW.HERITAGEISLAND.COM

For the Kids in Leinster

Altamont Gardens

Tullow, Co. Carlow
Tel: 0503-59444   Fax: 0503-59510
www.heritageireland.com

- Open year round Monday to Friday,
  9:00 to 5:00; open weekends Easter
  to end of October, 2.00 to 5.30
- Adults, €2.90; Children, €1.30;
  Family, €7.40
- Located near Ballon, signposted off the
  N80 and N81 between Tullow and
  Bunclody

Large, beautiful old world garden,
Robinsonian in style with a strong
emphasis on the informal tradition of combining a good plant collection within the natural landscape of
its environment. Lawns and clipped yews slope down to a lake surrounded by rare trees and shrubs and a
profusion of roses, old and modern, and herbaceous plants scent the air. *An OPW site.*

Ballykeenan House Pet Farm and Aviary

Myshall, Co Carlow
Tel: 0509-9157665

- Open weekdays, 11.00 to 5.00, Sundays,
  2.00 to 5.00
- Adults, €3.00; Children, €2.00
- Located off the N80 Dublin/Rosslare road
  between Ballon and Kildavin
- Caters for children's parties
- Caters for school groups/tours

Ballykeenan House has over 100 different
species of birds, small and large animals
including ostrich, emu, llama, sheep, deer,
rabbits, hamsters and goats. They provide
guided tours and have an indoor picnic area.

Country Quads

Tinnecarrig, Borris, Co Carlow
Tel: 059-9724624   Fax: 059-9724624
countryquads@eircom.net   www.countryquads.com

- Open daily year round, 9.30 to 6.00
- Contact Country Quads for fee information
- Located near Borris, half an hour from Carlow and Kilkenny
- Caters for children's parties
- Caters for school groups/tours
- Special programmes for children

Ⓒ Ⓕ

Country Quads provides quad bike trekking in scenic countryside with hills, rivers, see-saw and other obstacles to make the journey more interesting. They cater for children from eight years up and up to 12 can travel in the same group. Clay-pigeon shooting is also available for groups of seven or more adults. The clubhouse provides showers and toilets and also has table tennis and a trampoline. Picnic and barbecue area available.

County Carlow Military Museum

Old Church, St Dympna's Hospital, Athy Road, Carlow
Tel: 087-2850509
www.countycarlowmilitarymuseum.com

- Open most Sundays from 2.00 to 5.00 from March 17 to end October
- Adults, €2.50; Children, €1.30
- Located in the Old Church Building in the ground of St Dympna's Hospital

County Carlow Military Museum was founded in 1995 and moved to its present location in July 2001. Among its displays are the uniforms of the Irish Defence Forces, UN peacekeeping missions in the Congo, Lebanon and Somalia, reconstruction of a World War I trench, and an exhibit on Carlow soldiers who have served in the military throughout the world.

Go with the Flow River Adventures

Tel: 087-2529700
info@gowiththeflow.ie   www.gowiththeflow.ie

- Open all year
- Fees: Telephone for information
- Located on the River Barrow near Borris, Co Carlow
- Caters for school groups/tours
- Suitable for children 9+

Go with the Flow River Adventures tailors their adventures towards each group offering a safe and exciting river experience for children and adults. They also provide canoe hire, instruction courses, canoe holiday planning and fundraising events.

Airfield Trust

Upper Kilmacud Road, Dundrum, Dublin 14
Tel: 01-2984301   Fax: 01-2962832
booking@airfield.ie   www.airfield.ie

- Open April to September, Tuesday to Sunday, 11.00 to 5.00
- Adults, €5.00; Children, €3.00; Family €18.00; Season Ticket, €50.00
- Located on Kilmacud Road Upper in Dundrum, just south of Dublin
- Caters for school groups/tours
- Special programmes for children

Airfield Gardens and Walk, which includes five acres of beautifully redesigned ornamental gardens and a market trail around 40 acres of farm and gardens, form part of the Airfield Trust, established in 1993 to administer the estate of the late Letitia and Naomi Overend. Today, following an extensive programme of restoration, Airfield is used as a centre for learning and recreation. Facilities include a classroom complex, arts and craft courtyard, archival reading room and full educational and cultural programme.

Ardgillan Demesne

Balbriggan, Co Dublin
Tel: 01-8492212   Fax: 01-8492786

- Castle open April to September, 11.00 to 6.00 Tuesday to Sunday and Public Holidays; October to March from 11.00 to 4.30; July and August open seven days
- Admission to Castle: Adults, €6.00; Students, €4.50; Family, €12.50. Group rates available
- Located off the N1 north of Dublin

🍽 ♿ 🚻

Ardgillan is situated on the elevated coastline between Balbriggan and Skerries, 20 miles north of Dublin City. It is unique among Dublin's Regional Parks for the magnificent views it enjoys of the coastline. The Park consists of 194 acres of rolling pasture land, mixed woodland and gardens, overlooking the Bay of Drogheda. The castle, built in 1738, consists of two storeys over a basement which extends out under the south lawns. The first floor area is used for an annual programme of exhibitions and is also the permanent home of the seventeenth-century "Down Survey of Ireland".

The Ark — A Cultural Centre for Children

Eustace Street, Temple Bar, Dublin 2
Tel: 01-6707788   Fax: 01-6707758
info@ark.ie   www.ark.ie

- Performances/workshops Monday to Friday during term; public performances on weekends and during holidays; ring for schedule
- Costs vary
- Located in Temple Bar
- Caters for school groups/tours
- Special programmes for children

♿ 🚻

The Ark is Europe's only custom-built cultural centre devoted to work for, by, with and about children. Approximately 30,000 children visit The Ark each year to participate in a variety of activities including drama and theatre festivals, concerts, music festivals, visual arts exhibitions and workshops. The Ark also fields several outreach initiatives including the Mobile Ark, the Healing Ark, ArkLink, the Virtual Ark and Arkimedia. Contact The Ark for details.

Bank of Ireland Arts Centre

Foster Place, College Green, Dublin 2
Tel: 01-6712261   Fax: 01-6707556
boiarts@boimail.com   www.bankofireland.ie

HeritageISLAND
IRELAND'S VISITOR ATTRACTIONS

- Open year round, Tuesday to Friday, 10.00 to 4.00
- Adults, €3.00; Children, €2.00; Family, €7.50
- Located at College Green in city centre
- Caters for school groups/tours

Bank of Ireland Arts Centre's programme "200 Years of History" is an interactive museum which reflects both Irish history and the history of banking over the past 200 years. It also traces the history of the adjoining College Green building, one of the architectural landmarks of Georgian Dublin, dating back to its former role as the Irish Houses of Parliament.

Bear Factory

Unit 3, Level 3
Dundrum Town Centre
Dublin 16
Tel: 01-2166825
www.bearfactory.co.uk

- Open Monday to Friday 10.00 to 9.00; Saturday 10.00 to 7.00; Sunday 12.00 to 6.00
- Admission free; costs vary
- Caters for children's parties
- Caters for school groups/tours
- Special programmes for children

Every Bear Factory offers a truly unique opportunity for children to participate in an entertaining, exciting, interactive experience where they can select and create their own unique furry friend, name them, give them a voice, buy outfits for them and take them home in their own gift box or "pet carrier". Bear Factory also offers party packages so that a whole group of children can enjoy the experience of creating their very own furry friend. School tours are a specialty.

The Casino
off Malahide Road, Marino, Dublin 3
Tel: 01-8331618   Fax: 01-8332636
www.heritageireland.ie

- Open daily June to September, 10.00 to 6.00; May, 10.00 to 5.00; rest of year, Saturday and Sunday from 12.00 to 4.00
- Adults, €2.90; Children, €1.30; Family, €7.40
- Located off the Malahide Road in Marino
- Entry by guided tour only

The Casino is considered to be one of the finest eighteenth-century neo-classical buildings in Europe. The Casino, meaning "small house", surprisingly contains 16 finely decorated rooms. The interior of the Casino is intricately decorated with ornate plasterwork and richly patterned marquetry floors. Outside it looks like a Greek temple with one room and one storey inside, but inside the Casino is a practical house with 16 rooms and three storeys. *An OPW site.*

Chester Beatty Library
Dublin Castle, Dublin 2
Tel: 01-4070750   Fax: 01-4070760
info@cbl.ie   www.cbl.ie

- Open year round Monday to Friday, 10.00 to 5.00, Saturday, 11.00 to 5.00, Sunday, 1.00 to 5.00 (closed Mondays from October to April)
- No entrance fee
- Located in Dublin Castle on Dame Street
- Caters for school groups/tours
- Special programmes for children

The Chester Beatty Library, European Museum of the Year in 2002 and one of Ireland's National Cultural Institutions, was created by Sir Alfred Chester Beatty and bequeathed by him to a trust for the benefit of the public. The Library is both an art museum and library, housing an outstanding collection of Islamic manuscripts, Chinese, Japanese, Indian and other Oriental art. Early papyri, including some of the earliest texts of the Bible and other early Christian manuscripts, western prints and printed books complete what is one of the richest collections of its kind in the world. Children's workshops run monthly and pre-booking is essential.

The Chimney Viewing Tower

Smithfield Village, Dublin 7
Tel: 01-8173800   Fax: 01-8173839
reservations@chiefoneills.com   www.chiefoneills.com

- Open Monday to Saturday, 10.00 to 5.00; Sundays, 11.00 to 5.30
- Adults, €5.00; Children, €3.50; Family, €10.00
- Located in Smithfield Village, 10 minutes' walk from O'Connell Street

🍴 ♿ 🚻 🎁

One of the most prominent features of Smithfield Village is the Chimney Viewing Tower. The existing 185-foot Jameson Distillery Chimney has been topped with a two-tiered glass-enclosed viewing platform, and provides a 360-degree panoramic view of Dublin city. The viewing platform is served by a glass lift which runs alongside the chimney. The Chimney can also be hired exclusively for private functions.

Christ Church Cathedral

Christchurch Place, Dublin 8
Tel: 01-6778099   Fax: 679-8991
administrator@cccdub.ie   www.cccdub.ie

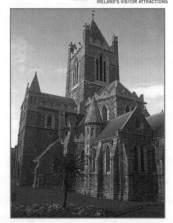

- Cathedral Visiting Hours: Monday to Friday, September to May, 9.45 to 5.00; June to August, 9.00 to 6.00; Saturday and Sunday (subject to services), 10.00 to 5.00.
- Treasures of Christ Church: Monday to Friday, 9.45 to 5.00; Saturday, 10.00 to 4.45; Sunday, 12.30 to 3.15
- Adults, €5.00; Students/OAP, €2.50; Children, free
- Located due west from Trinity College at the end of Dame Street and Lord Edward Street

Christ Church Cathedral, founded in the year 1030 by Sitric, King of the Dublin Norsemen, is Dublin's oldest building. Dating back to the eleventh century, the cathedral and the exhibition "Treasures of Christ Church" reflect 1,000 years of history, architecture and worship in Ireland. The choral services are sung by the cathedral choir, which traces its origins to the choir school founded in 1480 and is famous for taking part in the first performance of Handel's *Messiah*. "Treasures of Christ Church" displays a unique range of manuscripts, historic artefacts and spectacular examples of gold and silver ware.

Custom House Visitor Centre

Custom House Quay, Dublin 1
Tel: 01-8882538   Fax: 01-8882407

- Open mid-March to November, 10.00 to
  12.30, Monday to Friday, 2.00 to 5.00,
  Saturday and Sunday; November to mid-
  March, 10.00 to 12.30, Wednesday to Friday,
  2.00 to 5.00, Sunday
- Adults, €1.00; Students, free; Family, €3.00
- Located near Busaras, 5 minutes walk from
  O'Connell Bridge

The Custom House, designed by the renowned James Gandon, was completed in 1791 and is one of Dublin's finest heritage buildings. The Visitor Centre is located in and around the Dome or Clocktower area which contains the most important interior features to have survived the destruction of the building by fire in 1921 during one of the more dramatic events of the War of Independence. The Visitor Centre includes a Gandon Museum, the history of the Custom House itself, and important characters who have had offices in the building in the two centuries since it was completed.

Dalkey Castle and Heritage Museum

Castle Street, Dalkey, Co Dublin
Tel: 01-2858366   Fax: 01-2843141
diht@indigo.ie   www.dalkeycastle.com

HeritageISLAND
IRELAND'S VISITOR ATTRACTIONS

- Open year round, 9.30 to 5.00, Monday to Friday; Saturdays,
  Sundays and Public Holidays year round, 11.00 to 5.00
  (closed for lunch, 1.00 to 2.00)
- Adults, €6.00; Children, €4.00; Family, €16.00
- Located in Dalkey, 12.8 km south of Dublin

🍽 ♿ 🚻 🎁

Explore Goat Castle with its murder hole, bartizan garderobe, machicolations and battlements. View models of Medieval Dalkey, the Atmospheric and Funicular railways and the much-loved trams. Explore the folklore, customs and literary history of Dalkey, written by playwright Hugh Leonard. Visit 10th-century St. Begnet's Church and Graveyard. See the exhibition of James Joyce's Dalkey connections. Heritage Trails and Historical Walks begin from the Heritage Centre on selected days.

Drimnagh Castle

Long Mile Road, Drimnagh, Dublin 12
Tel: 01-4502530   Fax: 01-4508927
drimnaghcastle@eircom.net   www.iol.ie~drimnagh

- Open April 1 to September 30, Wednesday, Saturday, Sunday, 12.00 to 5.00; October 1 to March 31, Wednesdays, 12.00 to 5.00, Sundays, 2.00 to 5.00
- Adults, €4.00; Children, €2.00
- Located in Drimnagh, Dublin 12

Drimnagh Castle was, until 1954, one of the oldest continually inhabited castles in Ireland and is an outstanding example of an old feudal stronghold. It is the only Irish castle still to be surrounded by a flooded moat. The Castle consists of a Restored Great Hall and medieval undercroft, a tall battlement tower with lookout posts and other separate buildings. One of the most attractive aspects of Drimnagh is the garden – a formal seventeenth-century layout.

Dublin Castle

Dame Street, Dublin 2
Tel: 01-6777129   Fax: 01-6797831
tours@dublincastle.ie   www.dublincastle.ie

- Open Monday to Friday, 10.00 to 5.00; Sundays and Public Holidays, 2.00 to 5.00
- For guided tours: Adults, €4.50; Children,, €2.00
- Located on Dame Street, five minutes' walk from Trinity College

Dublin Castle is the heart of historic Dublin. In fact the city gets its name from the Black Pool, "Dubh linn", which was on the site of the present Castle Garden. The Castle stands on the ridge on a strategic site at the junction of the River Liffey and its tributary the Poddle, where the original fortification may have been an early Gaelic Ring Fort. Later a Viking fortress stood on this site, a portion of which is on view to visitors at the "Undercroft". The south range houses the magnificent State Apartments which were built as the residential quarters of the viceregal court. The State Apartments, Undercroft and Chapel Royal are open to visitors.

Dublin City Gallery The Hugh Lane

Charlemont House, Parnell Square North, Dublin 1
Tel: 01-2225550   Fax: 01-6722045
info.hughlane@dublincity.ie   www.hughlane.ie

- Open Tuesday to Thursday, 9.30 to 6.00; Friday and Saturday, 9.30 to 5.00; Sunday, 11.00 to 5.00
- No entrance fee to permanent collection; Admission to Francis Bacon Studio: Adults, €7.00 (€3.50 concessions); Under-18s, free
- Located on Parnell Square at the top of O'Connell St
- Caters for school groups/tours
- Special programmes for children

Located in Dublin's city centre, Dublin City Gallery The Hugh Lane houses one of Ireland's foremost collections of modern and contemporary art, including the reconstructed studio of Francis Bacon's Reece Mews Studio. The Gallery, which has undergone a major expansion and refurbishment, provides artist-led art workshops for children as well as drawing courses for teenagers. Picture guides, worksheets and basic drawing materials are available for children.

Dublin Civic Museum

58 South William Street, Dublin 2
Tel: 01-6794260
www.dublincitycouncil.ie

- Open Tuesday to Saturday, 10.00 to 6.00; Sunday, 11.00 to 2.00
- No entrance fee
- Located on South William Street in the city centre

The Dublin Civic Museum is housed in a historic building which was once the City Assembly House. A visitor to the museum will learn about a whole range of different aspects of life in Dublin through the ages from the exhibits which range from a collection of objects from Viking Dublin to a model of the Howth Tram. Subjects covered in the permanent collection include Streets and Buildings of Dublin, Traders, Industry, Transport, Political History, Maps and Views of Dublin.

Dublin Writers Museum

18 Parnell Square North, Dublin 1
Tel: 01-8722077   Fax: 01-8722231
writers@dublintourism.ie   www.visitdublin.ie

- Open Monday to Saturday, 10.00 to 5.00 (until 6.00 in summer); Sundays and Public Holidays, 11.00 to 5.00
- Adults, €6.70; Children, €4.20; Family, €19.00
- Located in Parnell Square, Dublin

The Irish literary tradition is one of the most illustrious in the world, famous for four Nobel Prize winners and for many other writers of international renown. In 1991 the Dublin Writers Museum was opened to house a history and celebration of literary Dublin. Situated in a magnificent eighteenth-century mansion in the north city centre, the collection features the lives and works of Dublin's literary celebrities over the past 300 years. Swift and Sheridan, Shaw and Wilde, Yeats, Joyce and Beckett are among those presented through their books, letters, portraits and personal items. The museum holds exhibitions and readings and has a special room devoted to children's literature.

Dublin Zoo

Phoenix Park, Dublin 8
Tel: 01-4748900   Fax: 01-6771660
info@dublinzoo.ie   www.dublinzoo.ie

- Open year round, Monday to Saturday, 9.30 to 6.00, Sunday, 10.30 to 6.00. Last entry 5.00
- Adults, €13.50; Children under 16, €9.00; Children under 3, free; Family tickets from €38.00 (concessions for the unwaged)
- Located in Phoenix Park, Dublin
- Caters for school groups/tours
- Special programmes for children

Just 3 km from the city centre, Dublin Zoo is set in 60 acres of landscaped grounds where animals and tropical birds from around the world can be seen. Highlights of the zoo include the World of Cats, Fringes of the Arctic, World of Primates and the 30-acre African Plains exhibit. There are also daily Meet the Keeper sessions, play areas, a Discovery Centre, zoo trains and much more.

Dublinia and the Viking World

St Michael's Hill, Christchurch, Dublin 8
Tel: 01-6794611   Fax: 01-6797116
info@dublinia.ie   www.dublinia.ie

Heritage**ISLAND**
IRELAND'S VISITOR ATTRACTIONS

- Open daily April to September 10.00 to 5.00; Monday to Saturday October to March, 11.00 to 4.00; Sundays/Bank holidays, 10.00 to 4.00
- Adults, €6.00, Children, €3.75 (under-fives free); Family, €16.00
- Located at Christ Church Cathedral in Dublin
- Caters for school groups/tours
- Special programmes for children

The award-winning permanent exhibition at Dublinia brings the turbulent history of medieval Dublin vividly to life. Visitors can step inside the medieval city and experience life in the Middle Ages at first hand — walk through the streets and laneways of the old city, take a shot at the man in the pillory, visit the Merchant's House and climb aboard ship at Wood Quay, try on a costume for size and try to lift a knight's shield and come face-to-face with the reconstructed image of a medieval woman.

Dublin's City Hall — The Story of the Capital

Dublin City Hall, Dame Street, Dublin 2
Tel: 01-6722204   Fax: 01-6722620
cityhall@dublincity.ie   www.dublincity.ie/cityhall

Heritage**ISLAND**
IRELAND'S VISITOR ATTRACTIONS

- Open Monday to Saturday, 10.00 to 5.15; Sundays and Bank Holidays, 2.00 to 5.00
- Adults, €4.00; Children, €1.50; Family, €10.00
- Located on Dame Street, 5 minutes from Trinity College

A multimedia exhibition tracing the evolution of the city from 1170 to the present day. The story is told through the display of Civic Regalia, including the Great City Sword, the Great Mace, the Lord Mayor's chain and city treasures, which are supported by computer interactives, archive films, models and costumes. Specially commissioned works of art depict aspects of the city's history. Located in City Hall, one of Dublin's finest neo-classical buildings which dates from 1779, this exhibition brings to life the changes in the city over the centuries.

Fort Lucan

Westmanstown, Lucan, Co Dublin
Tel: 01-6280166
jmartinsmith@eircom.net   www.fortlucan.com

- Open daily from May 17 to August 31, 10.00 to 6.00 (Sunday, 12.00 to 6.00); March 17 to May 12, open weekends and school holidays
- Adults, €3.00; Children, €9.00; group rates available
- Located in Lucan 1 mile from Clonsilla
- Caters for children's parties
- Caters for school groups/tours

Fort Lucan is a fully supervised adventure playground in County Dublin. There is a wide range of activities including 40-foot water slides, crazy golf, kart track, pendulum swings, aerial runway, trampolines, maze, high tower walks, a tots area and more.

Fry Model Railway

Malahide Castle Demesne, Malahide, Co Dublin
Tel: 01-8463779   Fax: 01-8463723
fryrailway@dublintourism.ie   www.visitdublin.com

- Open April to September, 10.00 to 5.00, Monday to Saturday; 2.00 to 6.00 Sundays and public holidays. Closed Fridays.
- Adults, €6.70; Children, €4.20; Family, €19.00
- Located at Malahide Castle, just outside Malahide Village

The Fry Model Railway is a unique collection of handmade models of Irish trains, from the beginning of rail travel to modern times. Situated in the beautiful grounds surrounding Malahide Castle, this delightful collection is a treat for railway enthusiasts, children and adults alike. The beautifully engineered models are from a collection originally built up in the 1920s and 1930s by Cyril Fry, a railway engineer and draughtsman, each piece assembled with the finest attention to detail. Irish and international exhibits from the earliest railway developments are run on a Grand Transport Complex which includes stations, bridges, trams, barges and even the river Liffey.

GAA Museum and Croke Park Stadium Tour

Croke Park, Dublin 3
Tel: 01-8558176   Fax: 01-8558104
gaamuseum@crokepark.ie   www.gaa.ie

HeritageISLAND
IRELAND'S VISITOR ATTRACTIONS

- Open all year, 9.30 to 5.00 Monday to Saturday; 12.00 to 5.00 Sundays
- Adults, €5.50 (€9.50 including tour); Children, €3.50 (€6.00 including tour); Family, €15.00 (€24.00 including tour)
- Located on the north side of Dublin, 15 minute walk from Connolly Station

The GAA Museum at Croke Park is designed to facilitate an experience of an integral part of Irish life and heritage through an exploration of its culture, history and unique national sports. Historic exhibits and touch-screen technology bring visitors the historic moments, the great names and games. Specially designed interactives allow visitors to test their skills in Ireland's most popular games. In addition to the Museum visitors may tour Croke Park, the home of Gaelic Games and the fourth largest stadium in Europe.

Gallery of Photography

Meeting House Square, Dublin 2
Tel: 01-6714654
gallery@irish-photography.com   www.irish-photography.com

- Open Tuesday to Saturday, 11.00 to 6.00; Sunday, 1.00 to 6.00
- No entrance fee
- Located between Eustace Street and Sycamore Street in Temple Bar
- Caters for school groups/tours

Since its inception in 1978 the Gallery of Photography has become Ireland's premier venue for photography. It has staged exhibitions with many of the major names in contemporary photography. The Gallery moved to its new location, a purpose-built space with fully fitted darkrooms in Meeting House Square in 1995. Groups are welcome to visit the Gallery. To arrange for a tour of the Gallery and an informal talk on the current exhibition, please contact the education officer.

Garda Museum/Archives

Record Tower, Dublin Castle, Dublin 2
Tel: 01-6669998   Fax: 01-6669992
gatower@iol.ie   www.policehistory.com

- Open daily, 9.30 to 4.30 (Saturday and Sunday may require appointment)
- No entrance fee
- Located on the grounds of Dublin Castle (pedestrians enter via Palace Street gate)
- Caters for school groups/tours

The museum contains a vast amount of archival and artefactual material relating to An Garda Síochána, Royal Irish Constabulary and the Dublin Metropolitan Police, including photos and other historical documents. The museum also houses a small research library.

Irish Jewish Museum

3 Walworth Road, off Victoria Street, Portobello, Dublin 8
Tel: 01-4901857 or 01-4531797

- Open May to September, Sunday, Tuesday and Thursday, 11.30 to 3.30; October and April, Sundays only, 10.30 to 2.30
- No entrance fee; donations appreciated
- Located off South Circular Road near the Grand Canal
- Caters for school groups/tours

The Irish-Jewish Museum is located in a former synagogue building with all its original features. The display includes memorabilia relating to the Jewish communities in Ireland, depicting their important, though small, place in Ireland's cultural and historical heritage. The collection includes photographs, paintings, certificates, books, letters and artefacts concerning all aspects of Jewish life. The display covers 150 years of professional, commercial and artistic activities and includes a gallery with Jewish religious objects. The original kitchen in the building recreates a typical Sabbath meal setting of the early 1900s. The museum was opened in 1985 by Irish-born President Chaim Herzog of Israel.

Irish Museum of Modern Art

Royal Hospital, Military Road, Kilmainham, Dublin 8
Tel: 01-6129900   Fax: 01-6129999
info@modernart.ie   www.modernart.ie

- Open Tuesday to Saturday, 10.00 to 5.30; Sundays and Bank Holidays, 12.00 to 5.30
- No entrance fee
- Located on Military Road in Kilmainham, five minutes from Heuston Station
- Caters for school groups/tours
- Special programmes for children

🍴 ♿ 🚻 🎁

The Irish Museum of Modern Art is Ireland's leading national institute for the collection and presentation of modern and contemporary art. The Museum's Education and Community Programme runs two programmes for children: *Explorer* is a family programme which provides an opportunity for children and adults to explore selected artworks together. The *Primary School Programme* is based around themes from a selected exhibition and includes a class visit with an art-making exercise for children in primary school. (See Featured Essay on page 56.)

The Iveagh Gardens

Clonmel Street, Dublin
Tel: 01-4757816
www.heritageireland.ie

- Open March to October, Monday to Saturday, 8.00 to 6.00; open daylight hours rest of year
- No entrance fee
- Located off Harcourt Street in Dublin (access also available from National Concert Grounds in Earlsfort Terrace)

The Iveagh Gardens are among the finest and least known of Dublin's parks and gardens. They were designed by Ninian Niven in 1863 and include a rustic grotto, cascade, fountains, maze, rosarium, archery grounds, wilderness and woodlands. An ongoing programme of restoration is taking place. *An OPW site.*

The James Joyce Centre

35 North Great George's Street, Dublin 1
Tel: 01-8788547   Fax: 01-8788488
joycecen@iol.ie   www.jamesjoyce.ie

- Open Monday to Saturday, 9.30 to 5.00; Sundays and Public Holidays, 12.30 to 5.00
- House tour: Adults, €5.00; Students, €4.00; Children under 12, free. Walking tour: Adults, €10.00; Students, €9.00; Children under 12, free
- Located on North Great George's St., near Parnell Square

The James Joyce Centre is dedicated to the promotion of an understanding of the life and works of this most famous Dubliner. It is located in a fine example of eighteenth-century Georgian Townhouse architecture, meticulously restored from a condition of dereliction. On permanent exhibit are a 1922 edition of *Ulysses* and the original door to number 7 Eccles Street, fictional home of Leopold Bloom, hero of *Ulysses*. The James Joyce Centre organises guided walks through Joycean Dublin taking in well-known sites from Joyce's books and personal life.

James Joyce Museum

Sandycove, Co Dublin
Tel: 01-2809265   Fax: 01-2809265
joycetower@dublintourism.ie   www.visitdublin.ie

- Open April to October, 10.00 to 5.00, Monday to Saturday; 2.00 to 6.00 Sundays; November to March, open by appointment
- Adults, €6.70; Children, €4.20; Family, €19.00
- Located eight miles south of Dublin on Coast Road

The James Joyce Tower was one of a series of Martello towers built to withstand an invasion by Napoleon and now holds a museum devoted to the life and works of James Joyce, who made the tower the setting for the first chapter of his masterpiece, *Ulysses*. Beautifully located eight miles south of Dublin on the coast road, this tower is the perfect setting for a museum dedicated to Joyce, a writer of international renown who remains, world-wide, the writer most associated with Dublin. The museum's collection includes letters, photographs, first and rare editions and personal possessions of Joyce, as well as items associated with the Dublin of *Ulysses*.

Kilmainham Gaol

Inchicore Road, Dublin 8
Tel: 01-4535984   Fax: 01-4532037
www.heritageireland.ie

- Open from April to September, Monday to Sunday, 9.30 to 5.00; October to March, Monday to Saturday, 9.30 to 4.00; Sunday, 10.00 to 5.00
- Adults, €5.30; Children/Students, €2.10; Family, €11.50
- Located in Inchicore, Dublin, 3.5 km from city centre
- Caters for school groups/tours

Kilmainham Gaol is one of the largest unoccupied gaols in Europe, covering some of the most heroic and tragic events in Ireland's emergence as a modern nation from 1780s to the 1920s. Attractions include a major exhibition detailing the political and penal history of the prison and its restoration. The tour of the prison includes an audio-visual show. Tours may be arranged for visitors with special needs by prior arrangement. *An OPW site.*

Lusk Heritage Centre

Lusk, Co Dublin
Tel: 01-8437683   Fax: 01-6616764
www.heritageireland.ie

- Open by prior arrangement. Please telephone number above or 01-6472461
- Adults, €1.60; Children, €1.00; Family, €4.50
- Located in centre of Lusk village

Lusk Heritage Centre is comprised of a round tower, a medieval belfry and a nineteenth-century church. They form a unit, although they were built over a period of almost 1,000 years. The belfry now houses an exhibition on medieval churches of North County Dublin and also the magnificent sixteenth-century effigy tomb of Sir Christopher Barnewall and his wife Marion Sharl. *An OPW site.*

Malahide Castle

Malahide, Co Dublin
Tel: 01-8462184   Fax: 01-8462537
malahidecastle@dublintourism.ie   www.visitdublin.ie

- Open 10.00 to 5.00, Monday to Saturday;
  Sundays and Public Holidays, 11.00 to 5.00
  (until 6.00 April to October); Closed for
  tours from 12.45 to 2.00
- Adults, €6.70; Children, €4.20; Family,
  €19.00
- Located just outside village of Malahide

Malahide Castle, set on 250 acres of parkland in the pretty seaside town of Malahide, was both a fortress and a private home for nearly 800 years and is an interesting mix of architectural styles. The house is furnished with beautiful period furniture together with an extensive collection of Irish portrait paintings, mainly from the National Gallery. Many additions and alterations have been made to this romantic and beautiful structure, but the contours of the surrounding parklands have changed little in 800 years, retaining a sense of the past. On the grounds is a very well-equipped children's playground.

Museum of Natural History

Merrion Street, Dublin 2
Tel: 01-6777444   Fax: 01-6619199
marketing@museum.ie   www.museum.ie

- Open year round, Tuesday to Saturday, 10.00 to 5.00;
  Sundays, 2.00 to 5.00
- No entrance fee
- Located in the city centre
- Caters for school groups/tours

The Museum of Natural History opened in 1857 just two years before Charles Darwin published his work "On the Origin of the Species". Packed with diverse animals from all walks of life, the Museum is a place where Darwin's theories of evolution and natural selection can be studied and understood. The Irish Room, located on the ground floor, is devoted largely to Irish mammals, birds, sea creatures and insects. The World Collection has as its centrepiece the skeleton of a 65-foot whale suspended from the roof. Other displays include a Giant Panda and a Pygmy Hippopotamus.

National Botanic Gardens

Glasnevin, Dublin 9
Tel: 01-8570909   Fax: 01-8360080
www.heritageireland.ie

- Open in summer, Monday to Saturday, 9.00 to 6.00; Sunday, 11.00 to 6.00. Open in winter, Monday to Saturday, 10.00 to 4.30; Sunday, 11.00 to 4.30
- No entrance fee
- Located on the south bank of the Tolka River in Glasnevin

The National Botanic Gardens, Glasnevin, were founded by the Royal Dublin Society in 1795. The Gardens contain many attractive features including an arboretum, rock garden and burren areas, large pond, extensive herbaceous borders, student garden and a rare example of Victorian carpet bedding. Glasshouses include the beautifully restored curvilinear range, alpine house and the complex for ferns, tropical water plants and succulents. *An OPW site.*

National Concert Hall

Earlsfort Terrace, Dublin
Tel: 01-4170077   Fax (box office): 01-4751507
info@nch.ie   www.nch.ie

- Box office hours: Monday to Saturday, 10.00 to 7.00
- No entrance fee. Fees for performances vary.
- Located in Dublin city centre

The National Concert Hall is Ireland's most prestigious music venue. The magnificent building was designed in the classical style for the Great Exhibition of 1865. As well as weekly performances by the NSOI, the National Concert Hall promotes a programme of visiting international artists and orchestras, as well as concerts of jazz, contemporary and traditional Irish music. In addition to this, its popular Education and Outreach Programme presents concerts and events for families and children throughout the year.

National Gallery of Ireland

Merrion Square and Clare Street, Dublin
Tel: 01-6615133   Fax: 01-6615372
info@ngi.ie   www.nationalgallery.ie

- Open year round, Monday to Saturday,
  9.30 to 5.30 (8.30 on Thursday);
  Sunday, 12.00 to 5.30
- No entrance fee
- Located in Dublin city centre

The National Gallery of Ireland was founded by an Act of Parliament in 1854 and opened to the public in 1864. In addition to the national collection of Irish art, the Gallery houses the national collection of European Old Master paintings. Access for visitors with disabilities to all public areas in the Gallery (lifts to all levels). Wheelchairs available on request. Tours for visually and hearing impaired visitors may be booked through the Education Department of the Gallery. There is a regular programme of art courses, workshops and outreach activities for adults, teenagers, children and families.

National Library of Ireland

Kildare Street, Dublin
Tel: 01-6030200   Fax: 01-6766650
www.nli.ie

- Open year round Monday to Wednesday,
  10.00 to 9.00; Thursday to Friday,
  10.00 to 5.00; Saturday, 10.00 to 1.00
- No entrance fee
- Located in Dublin city centre

The National Library of Ireland was founded in 1877 based on collections from The Royal Dublin Society. The National Library holds an estimated five million items. There are collections of printed books, manuscripts, prints and drawings, photos, maps, newspapers, microfilms and ephemera. The library's research facilities are open to all those with genuine research needs.

National Museum of Decorative Arts and History

Collins Barracks, Benburb Street, Dublin 7
Tel: 01-6777444   Fax: 01-6791025
education@museum.ie   www.museum.ie

- Open Tuesday to Saturday, 10.00 to 5.00, Sunday 2.00 to 5.00
- No entrance fee
- Located two km from City Centre
- Caters for children's parties
- Caters for school groups/tours
- Special programmes for children

The National Museum of Decorative Arts and History organises events for children and adults throughout the year, including talks, art workshops and demonstrations. Admission is free and all materials are provided. The "My Museum" programme runs every Sunday at 3.00pm, alternating between the National Museums of Archaeology and History, Natural History, and Decorative Arts and History. Some events are suitable for children as young as four.

National Museum of Ireland

Kildare Street, Dublin
Tel: 01-6777444   Fax: 01-6777872
marketing@museum.ie   www.museum.ie

- Open year round, Tuesday to Saturday, 10.00 to 5.00; Sunday, 2.00 to 5.00
- No entrance fee
- Located in Dublin city centre

Opened in 1890, the National Museum of Ireland contains artifacts dating from 7000 BC to the twentieth century. Prehistoric Ireland introduces the visitor to the everyday culture of prehistory. Viking Age Ireland focuses on Irish Archaeology from 800-1200 AD. The Road to Independence is a fascinating exhibition which deals with Irish history at the time of independence, 1916-1921. Ancient Egypt, the most recent addition to the range of exhibitions, gives visitors a glimpse of a multifaceted civilisation.

National Photographic Archive

Meeting House Square, Temple Bar, Dublin
Tel: 01-6030200   Fax: 01-6777451
www.nli.ie

- Open year round, Monday to Friday, 10.00 to 5.00;
  Saturday 10.00 to 2.00 (exhibition only)
- No entrance fee
- Located in Temple Bar in Dublin

👨 👩   🎁

The National Photographic Archive, which is part of the National Library of Ireland, was opened in 1998 in an award-winning building in Temple Bar. The archive holds an unrivalled collection of photographic images relating to Irish history, topography and cultural and social life. The collection is especially rich in late nineteenth and early twentieth century topographical views and studio portraits, but also includes photographs taken during the Rebellion of 1916 and the subsequent War of Independence and Civil War, as well as other historic events.

Number Twenty Nine

29 Fitzwilliam Street Lower, Dublin 2
Tel: 01-7026165
numbertwentynine@esb.ie   www.esb.ie/numbertwentynine

- Open Tuesday to Saturday, 10.00 to 5.00;
  Sunday, 1.00 to 5.00
- Adults, €4.50; Children under 16 free
- Located adjacent to Merrion Square
- Caters for school groups/tours

🍽 ♿ 👨 👩 🎁

Number Twenty Nine is Dublin's Georgian House Museum. Visitors take a guided tour from the basement to the attic, through rooms which have been furnished with original artefacts as they would have been in the years 1790 to 1820. The museum captures life in this period and presents an insight into the social, cultural and political life of the capital. Number Twenty Nine regularly runs educational and outreach events such as themed guided tours, special educational workshops, lecture series and targeted group-based activities.

Old Jameson Distillery

Bow Street, Smithfield Village, Dublin 7
Tel: 01-8072355   Fax: 01-8072369
reservations@ojd.ie   www.jamesondistillery.ie

HeritageISLAND
IRELAND'S VISITOR ATTRACTIONS

- Open daily year round, 9.30 to 6.00
- Adults, €8.75; Children, €3.95
- Located in Smithfield, one-half mile from city centre

The Old Jameson Distillery in Smithfield Village is in the heart of Old Dublin. Irish whiskey can trace its history back to the sixth century. Almost like a tour of a working distillery, visitors can follow the fascinating craft of whiskey-making through the different stages from grain intake to malting, mashing, fermentation, distillation, maturation and bottling. Finally, the tour culminates in the Jameson Bar for a traditional Irish whiskey-tasting session.

Pearse Museum

Nature Study Room, St Enda's Park,
Rathfarnham, Dublin 16
Tel: 01-4934218   Fax: 01-4936120
www.heritageireland.ie

- Opens at 10.00 Wednesday to Sunday
- No entrance fee
- Located on the Grange Road in Rathfarnham
- Caters for school groups/tours

The museum provides nature walks and other nature study activities through its Nature Study Centre for primary and secondary level children. The Pearse Museum is scheduled to close for major refurbishment in mid-2006 but the Nature Study Centre will remain open during the refurbishment period. *An OPW site.*

Phoenix Park Visitor Centre

Phoenix Park, Dublin 8
Tel: 01-6770095   Fax: 01-6770095
phoenixparkvisitorcentre@duchas.ie   www.heritageireland.ie

- Open daily April to September, 10.00 to 6.00 (until 5.00 in October); November to March, Saturday and Sunday, 10.00 to 5.00
- Adults, €2.90; Children, €1.30; Family, €7.40
- Located in Phoenix Park

🍴 ♿ 🚻

The Phoenix Park is one of the largest and most magnificent city parks in Europe. A lively and entertaining exhibition on the history and wildlife of the Phoenix Park is on display in the Visitor Centre. Here visitors can receive information and enjoy a historical interpretation of the park from 3500 BC to the present day. There is a special section for children which allows them to explore the wonders of forest life. Adjoining the Visitor Centre is the fully restored Ashtown Castle, a medieval tower house that probably dates from the seventeenth century. The Castle had been incorporated into a more modern house and was "rediscovered" when this building was demolished due to dry rot. *An OPW site.*

Rathfarnham Castle

Rathfarnham, Dublin 14
Tel: 01-4939462   Fax: 01-6616764
rathfarnhamcastle@opw.ie   www.heritageireland.ie

- Open daily May to October, 9.30 to 5.30
- Adults, €2.10; Children, €1.10; Family, €5.80
- Located in Rathfarnham

🍴 ♿ 🚻

Rathfarnham Castle has a very colourful and interesting history. The date of the foundation of the castle is uncertain but research would suggest 1583. It was built as a comfortable defensible residence and by the end of the sixteenth century it was acknowledged as one of the finest castles in County Dublin. Visitors to the castle can view eighteenth-century interiors by Sir William Chambers and James "Athenian" Stewart. The visitor can see tantalising glimpses of the layers of the castle's earlier existence during research. *An OPW site.*

Saint Patrick's Cathedral

Saint Patrick's Close, Dublin 8
Tel: 01-4539472   Fax: 01-4546374
admin@stpatrickscathedral.ie   www.stpatrickscathedral.ie

HeritageISLAND
IRELAND'S VISITOR ATTRACTIONS

- Open daily March to October, 9.00 to 6.00;
  November to February, Saturday, 9.00 to 5.00,
  Sunday, 9.00 to 3.00
- Adults, €5.00; Children, €4.00; Family, €12.00
- Located off Patrick Street

♀♂   🎁

Saint Patrick's Cathedral has contributed much to Irish life throughout its long history (it was founded in 1191). The writer and satirist Jonathan Swift was Dean from 1713–1747. Handel's *Messiah* received its first performance in 1742 sung by the combined choirs of Saint Patrick's and Christ Church. Music has played an integral part in the life of Saint Patrick's since its foundation and it is the only cathedral in these islands to sing two services every day. Living Stones, the cathedral's permanent exhibition, celebrates Saint Patrick's place in the life of the city, its history and its role at the dawn of the third millennium.

The Shaw Birthplace

33 Synge Street, Dublin 8
Tel: 01-4750854   Fax: 01-8722231
shawhouse@dublintourism.ie   www.visitdublin.com

- Open May to September, Monday to Friday, 10.00 to
  1.00 and 2.00 to 5.00; Saturdays and Sundays, 2.00 to
  5.00. Closed Wednesdays
- Adults, €6.70; Children, €4.20; Family, €19.00
- Located on Synge Street, 15 minutes' walk from St
  Stephen's Green

🍽 (summer only)   ♿   ♀♂

The "Author of Many Plays" is the simple accolade to George Bernard Shaw on the plaque outside his birthplace and his Victorian home and early life mirrors this simplicity. The first home of the Shaw family and the renowned playwright has been restored to its Victorian elegance and charm and has the appearance that the family have just gone out for the afternoon. The neat terraced house is as much a celebration of Victorian Dublin domestic life as of the early years of one of Dublin's Nobel Prize winners for literature.

Introducing Children to Contemporary Art

Helen O'Donoghue

A tiny dress sits, upright, perched up high on a glass shelf. How can it just sit there and not fall over? Is it frozen after a night outdoors on the clothes line? But it is not white with frost as washing usually is when it is taken from the clothes line on a frosty morning. It is red, a blood red, and the skirt is covered with berries, rosehips, shrivelled and blackened and the sparkles that I thought were sequins are in actual fact dressmaker's pins! Looking up from underneath, through the transparency of the glass shelf, I can see the hundreds of sharp pins massed inside the interior, each berry attached to the tiny shirt by a sharp straight pin!

What I am describing is *Berry Dress* made in 1994 by the Irish artist, Alice Maher. It is one of the thousands of artworks housed in the National Collection at the Irish Museum of Modern Art (IMMA).

Encountering contemporary works of art is exciting. But it can be challenging and sometimes puzzling and it always raises questions. Not only questions such as "what on earth is that?" or "is that art?" but broader philosophical questions. Artworks can act as a catalyst to unlock meaning in people. When I first encountered *Berry Dress* I recalled my childhood experiences of long summer days wearing hand-made cotton dresses, running across the fields behind our house and the bitter sweetness of the blackberries plucked from the hedgerows. Happy memories. But it also triggered uncomfortable memories of falling on bared knees on the rough ground as a result of running too fast or scary nights convincing myself that the shadows on the wall of my bedroom were not, in fact, ghosts coming to get me. Artworks are often delightful but also provocative.

Alice Maher often makes work based on her memories of her rural childhood in County Tipperary which she describes as not always being the romantic ideal of a rural childhood. When I saw this work for the first time I found myself transported back in time to my own experiences of childhood.

Observing children in IMMA's galleries over time has enriched my own experience of contemporary art and added rich meanings to my understanding of many of the artists' work that is exhibited.

Recalling children from our primary school's programmes explore an artwork created by another Irish artist, Kathy Prendergast, which she chose not to title, revealed the possibility of imaginative spaces that can be opened up for children.

This work was similar to Alice Maher's and was hung above the eye level of the average eight-year-old child. It is a hand-knitted, undyed baby's jumper. Children entering the gallery were excited and usually ran towards this to get a closer look but were suddenly halted and silenced by a tremor of a movement observed gently pulsating from under the jumper where a human heart might normally lie. After expressing their awe at this, the children quickly moved towards the wall to investigate what was the cause of this magical breathing and figuring out how it worked on peeping upwards among the folds of the jumper let out squeals of delight when they spotted the minute motor.

Immediately their imaginations were set alight. The artwork acted as a stimulus to set creativity in motion. A multitude of ideas about why this strange lonely jumper was mounted onto the wall emerged and each child was confident that he or she had the right answer. And each child had . . .

I will close with an extract from a poem written Kyle Petrie, a 4th class student from Rathfarnham, where he expresses his discovery of his imagination after investigating another artwork, *Large Head*, by the German artist Stephan Balkenhal:

"In My Head"

In my head where nobody goes!
In my head where nobody knows!
Wow there's my imagination box,
I wonder what's on . . .

Helen O'Donoghue is Head of Education and Community Programmes at the Irish Museum of Modern Art.

Skerries Mills

Skerries, Co Dublin
Tel: 01-8495208   Fax: 01-8495213
skerriesmills@indigo.ie   www.skerriesmills.org

- Open daily, April 1 to September 30, 10.30 to 5.30; October 1 to March 31, 10.30 to 4.30
- Admission is free. Charges for tours are Adults, €6.00; Children, €3.00; Family, €12.50
- Located in Skerries, five minutes' walk from train station
- Caters for school groups/tours

The Skerries Mills heritage centre and town park comprises a watermill, five-sail and four-sail windmills with association mill races, a mill pond and wetlands. The history of the mills can be traced to the early sixteenth century and a bakery was established on the site by 1840. The watermill and both windmills have been restored to working order and visitors can try their hand at grinding, read about the history of milling and observe the stones, shakers, sieves and elevators powered by wind or water.

St. Mary's Abbey

Chapter House, Meetinghouse Lane, Off Capel Street, Dublin
Tel: 01-8721490   Fax: 01-6613769
www.heritageireland.ie

- Open mid-June to mid-September, Wednesday and Sunday, 10.00 to 5.00
- Adults, €1.60; Children, €1.00; Family, €4.50
- Located off Capel Street in Dublin

The Abbey was founded in 1139 as a daughter house of the Benedictine Order of Savigny but became Cistercian in 1147. It was, until its suppression in the sixteenth century, one of the largest and most important monasteries in Ireland. The Heritage Service along with the Dublin Archaeological Society and the History of Art Department of Trinity College, Dublin have put together an interesting exhibition. Exhibition is accessed by stairs only. *An OPW site.*

Tara's Palace

Courtyard, Malahide Castle, Malahide, Co Dublin
Tel: 01-8463779   Fax: 01-8463723
www.malahidecastle.com

- Open April to September, Monday to Friday, 10.45 o 4.45; Saturdays, Sundays and Bank Holidays, 11.30 to 5.30. Closed Fridays
- Adults, €2.00; Children, €1.00 (all proceeds go to charities)
- Caters for school groups/tours

It is not widely known that Dublin has one of the world's greatest dolls' palaces — Tara's Palace in the courtyard of Malahide Castle. The dolls' palace is one-twelfth to scale and has been modelled on some of Ireland's greatest mansions. The palace is supported by many other historic dolls' houses, dolls and toys, including the earliest dolls' house in Ireland and the UK, as well as the dolls' house of Lady Wilde (Oscar's mother). The display is of great interest to children and families and is next door to the Fry Model Railway (see page 42). Tara's Palace is run by volunteers and all fees go to support children's charities.

Trinity College Library and Dublin Experience

College Street, Dublin 2
Tel: 01-6082308   Fax: 01-6082690
adiffley@tcd.ie   www.tcd.ie/library

Heritage ISLAND
IRELAND'S VISITOR ATTRACTIONS

- Open Monday to Saturday, 9.30 to 5.00, Sundays, 9.30 to 4.30 (October to May, 12.00 to 4.30)
- Library admission: Adults, €8.00; Dublin Experience admission: €5.00; Children free
- Located in the city centre
- Caters for school groups/tours

Trinity College Dublin, founded in 1592 by Queen Elizabeth I, is the oldest university in Ireland. The Old Library, built between 1712 and 1732, was renovated to coincide with the College's 400th anniversary in 1992. Visitor facilities include the Treasury, which houses the Book of Kells and other early Christian manuscripts; the Long Room, the largest single chamber library in the world containing 200,000 of the library's oldest books in its oak bookcases; and the Dublin Experience, located in the Arts Building, which is a multimedia representation of the history of Dublin from Viking times to the present day.

Viking Splash Tours

64 Patrick Street Dublin 8
Tel: 01-7076000
Viking@esatclear.ie   www.vikingsplashtours.com

- Open March to November, 10.00 to 5.00
- Adults, €16.00 (€18.50 in July and August); Children, €8.95 (€9.50 in July and August); Family tickets available
- Tour departs from Bull Alley Street by St Patrick's Cathedral, and from St Stephen's Green
- Caters for children's parties
- Caters for school groups/tours

Viking-costumed guides provide witty commentary on the sights of the city centre before splashing into water at Grand Canal Harbour to continue the tour. Visitors can wear Viking helmets on board and everyone learns how to do the Viking roar.

War Memorial Gardens

Islandbridge, Dublin
Tel: 01-6770236
www.heritageireland.ie

- Open year round, Monday to Friday, 8.00 to dusk; weekends, 10.00 to dusk
- No entrance fee
- Located on the South Circular Road.

These gardens are dedicated to the memory of 49,400 Irish soldiers who died in the 1914–1918 War. The names of all the soldiers are contained in the granite bookrooms in the Gardens. These gardens are not only a place of remembrance but are also of architectural interest and of great beauty. Designed by the famous architect Sir Edwin Lutyens (1869-1944), they are one of four gardens in Ireland designed by him, the others being Heywood Gardens, Lambay Island and those in Howth Castle. Sunken rose gardens, herbaceous borders and extensive tree planting make for an enjoyable visit in any season. *An OPW site.*

Castletown

Castletown, Celbridge, Co Kildare
Tel: 01-6288252   Fax: 01-6271811
www.heritageireland.ie

- Open Easter to end of September, Monday to
  Friday, 10.00 to 6.00; weekends, 1.00 to 6.00;
  October, Monday to Friday, 10.00 to 5.00;
  Sunday, 1.00 to 5.00; November, Sunday, 1.00
  to 5.00
- Adults, €3.70; Children, €1.30; Family, €8.70
- Located at the end of main street in Celbridge
- Caters for school groups/tours

Castletown is the largest and most significant Palladian-style country house in Ireland. Built c.1722 for the speaker of the Irish House of Commons, William Connolly, the entire estate was sold by the family in 1965 to the Hon. Desmond Guinness. Both Mr Guinness and subsequently the Castletown Foundation, which acquired the house in 1979, devoted considerable effort and resources to maintaining the house and restoring the principal rooms. Castletown was transferred to State care in 1994. *An OPW site.*

Irish National Stud, Japanese Gardens, St Fiachra's Garden and the Horse Museum

Tully, Kildare Town, Co Kildare
Tel: 045-521617   Fax: 045-522964
stud@irish-national-stud.ie   www.irish-national-stud.ie   HeritageISLAND
IRELAND'S VISITOR ATTRACTIONS

- Open daily February 12 to November 12, 9.30 to
  6.00; rest of year open for groups by request
- Adults, €9.00; Children, €4.50
- Located in Kildare, off the N7
- Caters for school groups/tours

The world-famous Japanese Gardens are situated in the 1,000-acre Tully estate, now known as The Irish National Stud. The gardens were laid out in their paths of beauty between 1906 and 1910 by Tassa Eida and his son Minoru, and have been carefully preserved as one of the gems of Ireland's heritage. St. Fiachra's Garden was created to celebrate the millennium. The centre of the garden is dominated by fissured limestone monastic cells and within these cells are hand-crafted Waterford Crystal rocks and plants such as ferns and orchids.

Kildare Town Heritage Centre

Market House, Market Square, Kildare
Tel: 045-530672
kildaretownheritagecen@ireland.com   www.kildare.ie/kildareheritagecentre

- Open May to September, Monday to Saturday, 9.30 to 5.30,; October to April, Monday to Friday, 10.00 to 5.00
- Contact Centre for admission fees
- Located at the square in town centre
- Caters for school groups/tours

Situated in the restored seventeenth-century market house is a multimedia exhibition telling the story of Kildare past and present. Cogitosus, a seventh-century monk, takes visitors on a fascinating journey through time — an audio-visual presentation of the town from when St. Brigid established her church in 480 AD, to later centuries when Kildare was raided by Vikings and ruled by Normans. Kildare gradually developed into a market town and a modern town while still preserving the outline of its street patterns, round tower and cathedral.

Larchill Arcadian Gardens

Dunshaughlin Road, Kilcock, Co Kildare
Tel: 01-6287354   Fax: 01-6284580
email@larchill.ie   www.larchill.ie

- Open daily (except Monday) from May to August, 12.00 to 6.00. Open weekends only in September
- Adults, €7.50; Children, €5.50; Family, €27.50
- Located five km from Kilcock on the Dunshaughlin Road
- Caters for children's parties
- Caters for school groups/tours
- Special programmes for children (please enquire)

Larchill is a 63-acre parklands garden with a lakeside walk, two-acre playground with old-fashioned games, wooden adventure trail, indoor play area, pondlife/nature studies, indoor Junior Science room, crazy croquet, large toddlers' sandpit, rare breeds of farm animals, pets' corner and a maze in the maize in mid-July and August. There are numerous family events and new for 2006 is an archery range with lessons.

Lullymore Heritage and Discovery Park

Lullymore, Rathangan, Co Kildare
Tel: 045-870238   Fax: 045-870238
lullypark@eircom.net   www.lullymorepark.com

- Open year round, daily 10.00 to 6.00;
- Individuals, €9.00; Family, €22.00
- Located in West Kildare outside Rathangan
- Caters for children's birthday parties
- Caters for school groups/tours
- Special programmes for children

L ullymore Heritage and Discovery Park offers a mixture of nature, heritage and fun for all ages. The story of the Irish people through the millennia unfolds in exhibits, replica settlements, Early Christian Visitor Centre, woodland/bog walkways and theme gardens. A new indoor play centre, "Funky Forest", was opened in 2005. Also on the grounds is Fionn McCumhaill's Adventure Park, which includes a purpose-built playground and 18-hole adventure golf course, as well as the Lullymore Road Train which brings visitors on a relaxing tour around the park.

Maynooth Castle

Maynooth, Co Kildare
Tel: 01-6286744   Fax: 01-6286848
maynoothcastle@opw.ie   www.heritageireland.ie

- Open June to end of September, Monday to Friday, 10.00 to 6.00; weekends, 1.00 to 6.00; open October, Sundays, 1.00 to 5.00
- No entrance fee
- Located at entrance to National University of Ireland, Maynooth at end of main street
- Caters for school groups/tours

M aynooth Castle was founded in the early thirteenth century and became the principal residence of the Kildare branch of the Geraldines. The Kildare FitzGeralds emerged as one of the most powerful families in Ireland with Maynooth Castle being one of the largest of the Earl's houses. The original Keep, constructed c. 1203, was one of the largest of its kind in Ireland. There is an exhibition on the history of the castle and family in the Keep. *An OPW site.*

Millennium Maze

Ballinafagh Farm, Prosperous, Co Kildare
Tel: 045-868151
info@themillenniummaze.com   www.themillenniummaze.com

- Open daily May to October, 12.00 to 6.00
- Contact Ballinafagh Farm for admission fees
- Located five km from Donadea Forest Park in North Kildare
- Caters for children's parties
- Caters for school groups/tours

The Millennium Maze was grown to mark the Millennium and is designed in the shape of a St Brigid's Cross. The fully grown hedge maze covers approximately one acre with more than 1.5 miles of paths, with hedges over six feet high. For the younger visitor and those less adventurous there is the paved maze, equally challenging but not enclosed. Children can visit the pets' corner to see and touch hens, rabbits, sheep, lambs and other animals. Other attractions include our crazy golf course, a sand pit for the toddlers and mystery puzzles.

The Steam Museum

Straffan, Co Kildare
Tel: 01-6273155   Fax: 01-6273477
sm@steam-museum.ie   www.steam-museum.ie

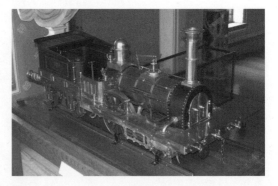

- Open June to August, Wednesday to Sunday, 2.00 to 6.00; May and September, open by appointment
- Adults, €7.50; Children, €5.00; Family, €20.00
- Located in Straffan on N7
- Caters for school groups/tours

The Steam Museum Building revives to use the magnificent Gothic pitch pine roof, stone window tracery and architectural features of the GS & WR Medieval Revival Church of St Jude, moved from Inchicore, Dublin. The Power Hall exhibits unique, stationary Steam Engines from the 1830s. Now saved from destruction and fully restored to working order, they turn under steam and once powered the Industrial Revolution. The Model Hall displays the Richard Guinness Collection of Inventors and early large size Prototype Railway Models. There is also Transatlantic Cable Memorabilia and an interactive area.

Straffan Butterfly Farm

Ovidstown, Straffan, Co Kildare
Tel: 01-6271109
info@straffanbutterflyfarm.com   www.straffanbutterflyfarm.com

- Open daily June to August, 12.00 to 5.30 (tours by appointment)
- Adults, €7.00; Children, €4.00; Family, €20.00
- Signposted from Kill on the Naas Road
- Caters for children's parties
- Caters for school groups/tours
- Special programmes for children

Whatever the weather, visitors to the Straffan Butterfly Farm can walk through a tropical greenhouse with spectacular butterflies flying and feeding all around them. Safe behind glass, visitors can see giant spiders, scorpions and small reptiles in natural surroundings. Exhibits in the educational display area depict the life cycles of butterflies and moths.

Dunmore Cave

Ballyfoyle, Co Kilkenny
Tel: 056-67726
www.heritageireland.ie

- Open daily mid-June to mid-September, 9.30 to 6.30; mid-March to mid June and mid-September to October, 10.00 to 5.00
- Adults, €2.90; Chlidren, €1.30; Family, €7.40
- Located 10 km from Kilkenny off N78

History and geology blend at Dunmore Cave to give an interesting and unique situation. Consisting of a series of chambers formed over millions of years, the cave contains some of the finest calcite formations found in any Irish cave. The cave has been known to man for many centuries and is first mentioned in the ninth-century Irish Triads. The most interesting reference, however, comes from the Annals which tells of a Viking massacre at the cave in the year 928 AD. Exhibitions and displays in the Visitor Centre. The cave is inaccessible for wheelchair users. *An OPW site.*

Jerpoint Abbey

Thomastown, Co Kilkenny
Tel: 056-24623   Fax: 056-54003
www.heritageireland.com

- Open daily March 1 to May 31, 10.00 to.
  5.00; June to mid-September, 9.30 to
  6.30; mid-September to November,
  10.00 to 5.00
- Adults, €2.90; Children, €1.30; Family,
  €7.40
- Located 2.5 km SW from Thomastown on
  N9

Jerpoint is an outstanding Cistercian abbey founded in the second half of the twelfth century. The church with its Romanesque details dates from this period. In the transept chapels the visitor can see thirteenth-sixteenth century tomb sculpture. The tower and cloister date from the fifteenth century. The chief delight of the Abbey is the sculptured cloister arcade with unique carvings. The Visitor Centre houses an interesting exhibition. Guided tours available. *An OPW site.*

Kilkenny Castle

Kilkenny City
Tel: 056-21450   Fax: 056-63488
www.heritageireland.com

- Open daily April to May, 10.30 to 5.00; June
  to August, 9.30 to 7.00; September, 10.00
  to 6.30; October to March, 10.30 to 12.45
  and 2.00 to 5.00
- Adults, €5.30; Children/Students, €2.10;
  Family, $11.50
- Located in centre of Kilkenny City

Kilkenny Castle, a twelfth-century castle remodelled in Victorian times and set in extensive parklands, was the principal seat of the Butler family, Marquesses and Dukes of Ormonde. Due to major restoration works, the central block now includes a library, drawing room, and bedrooms decorated in 1830's splendour as well as the beautiful Long Gallery. A suite of former servants' rooms is now the Butler Art Gallery, which mounts frequently changing exhibitions of contemporary art. Access for visitors with disabilities to ground floor and park/gardens only, where the playground includes play swings for children with disabilities. *An OPW site.*

Kilkenny Castle Park

The Parade, Kilkenny
Tel: 056-21450   Fax: 056-63488
www.heritageireland.com

- Open daily year round, 9.00 to 8.30 in summer; 9.00 to 4.30 in winter
- No entrance fee to park (fee to visit Kilkenny Castle)

♀ ♀

The Castle Park includes all the walled demesne parkland to the south and the formal terraced gardens to the north comprising a total of 50 acres. The terraced garden has been restored as a rose garden with formal beds of roses around a fountain. In the parkland paths lead to a small burial ground, a woodland walk and lake area and a children's playground. The playground is comprised of a small adventure unit for younger children and a larger unit for children up to 12.

Nore Valley Park Open Farm

Bennettsbridge, Kilkenny
Tel: 056-7727229   Fax: 056-7727747
norevalleypark@eircom.net   www.homepage.eircom.net/~norevalleypark/farm

- Open March 1 to September 30, Monday to Saturday, 9.00 to 8.00
- Entrance fee: €4.30 per person
- Located three km from Bennetsbridge off the R700
- Caters for children's parties
- Caters for school groups/tours
- Special programmes for children

🍽 ♿ ♀ ♀ 🎁

At Nore Valley Park Open Farm children can cuddle a rabbit or baby chick, bottle feed pet lambs or goats, identify crops, vegetables and trees, see tadpoles and frogs and a wide range of commercial and small farm animals. There is also crazy golf, pedal go-karts, trailer rides, an American-style fort, a 3D indoor maze, straw bounce and slides and a picnic area.

St. Mary's Church

Gowran, Co Kilkenny
Tel: 056-7226894
www.heritageireland.ie

- Contact Dúchas for opening times
- Contact Dúchas for admission fees
- Located in village of Gowran

This church was built in the late thirteenth century on the site of an earlier monastery. It was served by a "college" — clerics who lived in a community but who did not submit to the rule of a monastery. The church was a large and elaborate structure, with an aisled nave (the main part of the church where the congregation sat) and a long chancel (the section of the church where the altar was placed) and has high-quality architectural sculpture used throughout. In the late Middle Ages a massive tower was inserted between the nave and chancel, and in the nineteenth century this tower was incorporated into the parish church which was built in place of the chancel and which now takes up about half of the building. *An OPW site.*

Emo Court

Emo, Co Laois
Tel: 0502-26573   Fax: 0502-26573
www.heritageireland.com

- House open daily mid-June to mid-September, Tuesday to Sunday, 12.00 to 6.30; Gardens open year round during daylight hours
- Adults, €2.90; Children, €1.30; Family, €7.40
- Located 2.5 km from Emo (accessed from Kildare-Portlaoise Road (N7)).

Emo Court was designed by the architect James Gandon in 1790 for the Earls of Portarlington and is a magnificent example of the neo-classical style. During the middle of the twentieth century it was owned by the Jesuits, and was then acquired and extensively restored by Mr. Cholmeley-Harrison in the 1960s. The house is surrounded by beautiful gardens and parkland which were first laid out in the eighteenth century and contain formal lawns, a lake and woodland walks with many very fine trees and shrubs. The house and gardens were taken into State ownership in 1994. *An OPW site.*

Heywood Gardens
Ballinakill, Co Laois
Tel: 0502-33563
www.heritageireland.ie

- Open during daylight hours
- No entrance fee
- Located seven km SE from Abbeyleix off R432

Completed in 1912, the property consists of gardens, lakes, woodland and architectural features. It was transferred to State ownership in November 1993 from the Salesian Fathers who had taken care of it since 1941. The formal Gardens form the centrepiece of the property and were designed by the famous architect, Sir Edwin Lutyens (1869-1944) and probably landscaped by Gertrude Jekyll (1843-1932). It is one of four Gardens in this country designed by him, the others being in the War Memorial Park, Lambay Island and Howth Castle. The Gardens are composed of four elements linked by a terrace that ran along the front of the house which now no longer exists. There is limited access for visitors with disabilities. *An OPW site.*

Irish Fly Fishing and Game Shooting Museum
Attana House, Attanagh
Portlaoise, Co. Laois
Tel: 0502-36112
info@irishfishingandhuntingmuseum.com   www.irishfishingandhuntingmuseum.com

- Open daily all year from 10.00 to 6.00
- Adults, €5.00; Children, €2.00
- Located five minutes off the main Dublin—Cork road, N8, between Abbeyleix and Durrow

The Irish Fly Fishing and Game Shooting Museum is housed in an old farmhouse in Attanagh, a quaint village in County Laois, and has a collection of over 5,000 artefacts. It is the only museum of its kind in Ireland presenting and interpreting fishing and shooting and country life activities. It provides a history of the rich heritage of the Irish countryside. The aim of the museum is to collect, preserve, exhibit and interpret the equipment and tactics of fishing and shooting.

Corlea Trackway Visitor Centre

Kenagh, Co Longford
Tel: 043-22386   Fax: 043-22442
www.heritageireland.ie

- Open daily April to September 10.00 to 6.00
- Adults, €3.70; Children, €1.30; Family, €8.70
- Located three km from Kenagh Village and accessed from the Longford-Kenagh Road R397 (15 km from Longford)

The Centre interprets an Iron Age bog road which was built in the year 148 BC across the boglands close to the River Shannon. The oak road is the largest of its kind to have been uncovered in Europe and was excavated over the years by Professor Barry Raftery of University College Dublin. Inside the building, an 18-metre stretch of preserved road is on permanent display in a specially designed hall with humidifiers to prevent the ancient wood from cracking in the heat. *An OPW site.*

County Museum Dundalk

Jocelyn Street, Dundalk, Co Louth
Tel: 042-9327056
dlkmuseum1@eircom.net   www.dundalktown.ie

- Open daily May to October, 10.00 to 6.00
- Adults, €3.80; Children, €1.25;
- Located in Dundalk city centre

The County Museum, Dundalk is one of Ireland's finest local authority museums. Opened in 1994 the museum is located in a lovingly restored eighteenth-century distillery. The distillery once boasted the tallest chimney in Ireland, but unfortunately could not draw smoke. The museum boasts a variety of interesting artefacts, most notably a Heinkel bubble car located on the ground floor gallery as well as a leather coat reputed to have been worn by King William of Orange at the Battle of the Boyne.

Old Mellifont Abbey

Tullyallen, Drogheda, Co Louth
Tel: 041-9826459 Fax: 041-9826053
www.heritageireland.ie

- Open daily May to October, 10.00 to 6.00
- Adults, €2.10; Children, €1.10; Family, €5.80
- Located 1.5 km off Drogheda–Collon road

The first Cistercian monastery in Ireland, founded in 1142 by St Malachy of Armagh, its most unusual feature is the octagonal Lavabo c.1200. The Visitor Centre houses an interesting exhibition on the work of masons in the Middle Ages with fine examples of their craft on display. Access to site by stone stairway. Access for people with disabilities to the Visitor Centre. *An OPW site.*

Be Irish for a Day!

Causey Farm, Girley, Fordstown, Navan, Co Meath
Tel: 046-9434135
info@causeyexperience.com www.causeyexperience.com

- Open April to October, Monday to Saturday, for groups; check for availability for individuals
- Costs: €10.00 to €45.00 depending on options
- Located off the Kells–Athboy road in Co Meath
- Caters for school groups/tours
- Special programmes for children

Be Irish for a Day at the Causey Farm provides a hands-on insight into life with an Irish farming family. Children will learn how to cut turf, make brown bread, play hurling, work a sheepdog, dance a jig, make a súgan rope, milk a cow, play a bodhrán, enjoy a traditional Irish Céilí and much more. Also on the farm are treasure hunts, clay modelling, nature trails and a chance to meet farmyard friends.

Brú na Bóinne Visitors Centre (Knowth and Newgrange)
Donore, Co Meath
041-9880300   Fax: 041-9823071
www.heritageireland.ie

- Open June to mid-September, 9.00 to 7.00; open 9.30 to 5.00 in winter
- Admission to the Visitor Centre: Adults, €2.90; Children, €1.60; Family, €7.40; Admission to Centre and Newgrange: Adults, €5.80; Children, €2.90; Family, €14.00. Admission to Centre and Knowth: Adults, €4.50; Children, €1.60; Family, €11.00.
- Located between Slane and Drogheda on the Boyne
- Caters for school groups/tours

Brú na Bóinne Visitor Centre is designed to present the archaeological heritage of the Boyne Valley, which includes the megalithic passage tombs of Newgrange and Knowth. The Centre is the starting point for all visits to both monuments, and contains extensive interpretative displays and viewing areas. Special events are held on National Children's Day (first Sunday in October) and during Craft in Action Children's Week (last week in August). *An OPW site.*

Grove Garden and Tropical Bird Sanctuary
Kells, Co Meath
Tel: 046-34276   Fax: 046-34970
grove@iolfree.ie

- Open daily from March 17 to September 30, 10.00 to 6.00
- Adults, €6.00; Children, €3.50; Family, €20.00
- Located halfway between Kells and Athboy on R164
- Caters for children's parties

Grove Gardens has earned an international reputation as one of the premier garden attractions in the country. Covering four acres, the garden includes magnificent herbaceous borders, alpines and a large collection of roses and clematis. Children will enjoy the tropical bird garden and mini-zoo where they will be entertained by monkeys, camel, wallabies, racoons, owls and many other different species of tropical birds and animals.

Hill of Tara
Navan, Co Meath
Tel: 046-9025903   Fax: 046-9025903
www.heritageireland.ie

- Open daily from May 1 to September 30, 10.00 to 6.00
- Adults, €2.10; Children, €1.10; Family, €5.80
- Located off the N3 about 6 miles south of Navan
- Caters for school groups/tours

🍽 👫 🎁

Though best known as the seat of the High Kings of Ireland, the Hill of Tara has been an important site since the late Stone Age when a passage-tomb was constructed there. Tara was at the height of its power as a political and religious centre in the early centuries after Christ. Attractions include an audio-visual show and guided tours of the site. As much of the tour is outdoors, visitors are advised to wear protective clothing and shoes suitable for walking over uneven terrain. *An OPW site.*

Kells Heritage Centre
The Courthouse, Headfort Place, Kells, Co Meath
Tel: 046-9247840   Fax: 046-9247864
kellsheritagecentre@eircom.net   www.meathtourism.ie   HeritageISLAND
IRELAND'S VISITOR ATTRACTIONS

- Open May to September, Monday to Saturday, 10.00 to 5.30, Sundays, 2.00 to 6.00; open October to April, Monday to Saturday, 10.00 to 5.00
- Adults, €4,00; Children, €3.00; Family, €12.00
- Located in Kells on the Navan-Dublin road (N3)

🍽 ♿ 👫 🎁

Kells Heritage Centre is a vibrant visitor attraction located in the beautifully restored courthouse in Kells. The exhibition, entitled "The Splendour of Ireland", gives an insight into the crafts and culture of monastic Ireland and entices the visitor to explore the various sites of interest throughout the modern streetscape of Kells. The exhibition comprises four main sections: audio-visual presentation, The Crosses of Ireland, The Book of Kells and Monasticism in Ireland and Kells.

Loughcrew Historic Gardens

Oldcastle, Co Meath
Tel: 049-8541356   Fax: 049-8541921
info@loughcrew.com   www.loughcrew.com

- Open April 1 to August 31, 12.00 to 6.00; September 1 to March 31, 12.30 to 5.30. Tours available outside these hours.
- Adults, €6.00; Children, €3.50; Family, €18.00
- Located five km from Oldcastle off the Mullingar road

🍴 ♿ 🚻 🎁

History, beauty, fantasy and atmosphere make Loughcrew a magical experience. In a pleasure-garden of vistas and unexpected features, a spirit of mystery and dark history is created by the mighty ancient yew walk, a medieval mote and the martyr St Oliver Plunkett's family church. Children particularly enjoy the Watermill cascade, hidden reptiles and faeries, giant bugs and spiders lurking in trees, the "grotesque" grotto with grassy roof and the playground next to the log-built reception centre.

Newgrange Farm

Newgrange, Slane, Co Meath
Tel: 041-9824119
www.newgrangefarm.com

- Open Easter Saturday to August 31, 10.00 to 5.30
- Admission: €7.00 per person; group rates available
- Located off the N51 3 miles from Slane.
- Caters for children's parties
- Caters for school groups/tours

🍴 ♿ 🚻 🎁

Newgrange Farm is a 333-acre farm that surrounds the famous national monument of Newgrange. This is a family-owned working farm/educational facility that provides hands-on experience of bottle-feeding, holding, petting and seeing all the usual farm animals and poultry and much more. There are also tractor and rocking horse play areas, sand pits, and the occasional sheep race.

Sonairte – The National Ecology Centre

The Ninch, Laytown, Co Meath
Tel: 041-9827572
info@sonairte.org   www.sonairte.org

- Open weekends April to September, 10.30 to 5.00; ring for details out-of-season
- Adults, €3.00; Children, €1.00; Family, €6.00
- Sonairte is located 25 miles north of Dublin, between Julianstown and Laytown, just off the main N1 road.
- Caters for school groups/tours

Sonairte is Ireland's premier environmental education and visitor centre. Its goals are to promote increased awareness through the provision of innovative environmental education and practical demonstration in fields such as renewable energy, nature conservation and organics. Sonairte is particularly active in environmental education for children of school age, offering enlightening programmes and a first-class venue for school tours. Farmers' market on the third Sunday of every month.

Trim Castle

Trim, Co Meath
Tel: 046-9438619   Fax: 046-9438618
www.heritageireland.ie

- Open daily May to October, 10.00 to 6.00
- Adults, €3.70; Children, €1.30; Family, €8.70
- Located in village of Trim

Trim Castle is the largest Anglo-Norman castle in Ireland. Hugh de Lacy began construction of the castle in about 1172 but the central tower – the keep – was not completed until the 1220s. This 20-sided tower is three storeys high and was protected by a ditch, a curtain wall and a moat. Inside the tower were living quarters, a great hall and a small chapel. The Towngate had a portcullis to protect it as well as a "murder hole". The other gate, the Dublingate, has a barbican projecting from the tower. Originally the barbican spanned the water-filled moat which surrounded the curtain wall and had a drawbridge which was operated from above. *An OPW site.*

Trim Heritage Town
Castle Street, Trim, Co Meath
Tel: 046-9437227   Fax: 046-9438053
trimvisitorcentre@eircom.net   www.meathtourism.ie

Heritage**ISLAND**
IRELAND'S VISITOR ATTRACTIONS

- Open all year, 10.00 to 5.00, Sundays, 12.00 to 5.30
- Admission is free to the Centre. Audio-Visual fees: Adults, €3.20; Children, €1.90; Family, €8.90
- Located beside Trim Castle

The Trim Visitor Centre has an exciting multimedia exhibition, "The Power and the Glory", which paints a vivid picture of the historical background of the magnificent medieval ruins of Trim. Chroniclers, knights and kings emerge through the mists of time to recount the tale of the coming of the Normans to Trim, and of their astonishing influence which revolutionised Irish towns, farms and government.

Birr Castle Demesne and Ireland's Historic Science Centre
Birr, Co Offaly
Tel: 0509-20336   Fax: 0509-21583
mail@birrcastle.com   www.birrcastle.com

Heritage**ISLAND**
IRELAND'S VISITOR ATTRACTIONS

- Open daily March 16 to October, 9.00 to 6.00, November to March 15, 10.00 to 4.00
- Adults, €9.00; Children, €5.00; Family, €24.00
- Caters for school groups/tours
- Special programmes for children

Birr Castle Demesne and Science Centre includes the largest gardens in the country, an award-winning science centre and a 150-year-old telescope which was the largest in the world for 70 years and still looks and moves as it did then. There is a Discover Primary Science programme for primary students and a Junior Science Trail for secondary students.

Clonmacnoise

Shannonbridge, Co Offaly
Tel: 090-9674195   Fax: 090-9674273
www.heritageireland.com

- Open daily November to mid March, 10.00 to 5.30; mid-March to mid-May, 10.00 to 6.00; mid-May to early September, 9.00 to 7.00; September to October, 10.00 to 6.00
- Adults, €5.30; Children, €2.10; Family, €11.50
- Located 21 km from Athlone signposted from the N62

Clonmacnoise is an early Christian site founded by Saint Ciaran in the sixth century on the banks of the Shannon. The site includes the ruins of a cathedral, eight churches (tenth to thirteenth centuries), two round towers, three high crosses and a large collection of early Christian grave slabs. The original high crosses and grave slabs are on display in the Visitor Centre. There is an audio-visual show as well as a number of exhibitions. *An OPW site.*

Tullamore Dew Heritage Centre

Bury Quay, Tullamore, Co Offaly
Tel: 0506-25015   Fax: 0506-25016
tullamoredhc@eircom.net   www.tullamore-dew.org

HeritageISLAND
IRELAND'S VISITOR ATTRACTIONS

- Open Monday to Saturday, 9.00 to 6.00 (10.00 to 5.00 October to April); Sundays, 12.00 to 5.00
- Adults, €6.00; Children, €3.20
- Located off the main N6 Dublin-Galway road
- Caters for children's parties
- Caters for school groups/tours
- Special programmes for children

The Tullamore Dew Heritage Centre explores Tullamore's development from the small beginnings in the 1620s when there was just a castle, water mill and a few cottages, to the thriving midlands county town it is today, as well as the story of Tullamore's most famous products, Tullamore Dew Irish Whiskey and Irish Mist Liqueur. An educational programme for children includes guided tours, a worksheet, workshops and lectures. There is also a Fun Trail for children who receive a Certificate of Accomplishment after its completion.

Athlone Castle Visitor Centre

St Peter's Square, Athlone, Co Westmeath
Tel: 090-6442100   Fax: 090-6472100
jwalsh@athloneudc.ie   www.athlone.ie

- Open Easter to early October, first showing, 10.00; last showing, 4.30
- Adults, €5.50; Children, €1.60
- Located in centre of Athlone town
- Caters for school groups/tours

This Norman Castle dominates the town centre and commands the traditional gateway to the west of Ireland. The Visitor Centre features exhibitions and audio-visual presentations on the siege of Athlone, Count John McCormack, River Shannon wildlife and history with folk and military museums.

Belvedere House, Gardens and Park

Mullingar, Co Westmeath
Tel: 044-49060   Fax: 044-49002
info@belvedere-house.ie   www.belvedere-house.ie

- Open May to August, 9.30 to 9.00 (House, shop and café close at 6.00); March to April, September to October, 10.30 to 7.00 (House, shop and café close at 6.00)
- Adults, €8.75; Children, €4.75; Family, €24.00
- Located three miles from Mullingar on the N52

Belvedere House is a superb 160-acre estate on the shores of Lough Ennell, comprising an eighteenth-century hunting lodge, walled garden and landscaped park. Set within Belvedere's converted stable block is a Visitor Centre with a multimedia exhibition recounting the evocative eighteenth century story of the Wicked Earl, the history of the estate and its restoration. The grounds also include a Children's Play Area, Animal Sanctuary and the Belvedere Tram.

Clonmacnoise and West Offaly Railway

Blackwater Works, Shannonbridge, Athlone, Co Westmeath
Tel: 090-9674450   Fax: 090-9674210
bograil@bnm.ie   www.bnm.ie

- Open April, May, September, Monday to Friday, 10.00 to 5.00; June, July, August, 7 days a week, 10.00 to 5.00
- Adults, €6.50; Children, €4.80; Family, €22.00
- Located on the R357
- Caters for children's parties
- Caters for school groups/tours

People looking for something different should visit the Clonmacnoise and West Offaly Railway and enjoy a 5.5 mile fully guided rail tour through Blackwater bog. Visitors can learn about the flora, fauna and archaeology of the area and learn the answers to such questions as: What happens to bodies found buried in the bog? Are there any carnivorous plants found on the bogs? What is the record for cutting sods of turf per minute? How do we make electricity from the bog? Visitors can also stop off along the route to see a demonstration of how turf was cut by hand. Please phone ahead to check tour availability.

Glendeer Pet Farm

Drum, Athlone, Co Westmeath
Tel: 0906-437147   Fax: 096-437951
glendeere@glendeer.com   www.glendeer.com

- Open Monday to Saturday, 11.00 to 6.00; Sunday, 12.00 to 6.00
- Entrance fee: €7.00 per person
- Located four miles from Athlone off Dublin-Galway road
- Caters for children's parties
- Caters for school groups/tours

Glendeer is a six-acre open farm with over 50 species of animals and birds. Children can feed the pet animals which include deer, Vietnamese pot belly pigs, emu, ostrich, ponies, donkeys, Jersey cows, Anglo Nubian goats, peacocks and other rare birds and domestic fowl. There is also a picnic area, nature walk and children's play area. In December children can visit Ireland's Lapland, an all-weather facility which includes a visit with Santa and Dancer and Prancer, a crib and much more.

Lockes Distillery Museum

Kilbeggan, Co Westmeath
Tel: 057-9332134
lockesmuseum@iol.ie   www.lockesdistillerymuseum.com

- Open daily April to October, 9.00 to 6.00; November to March, 10.00 to 4.00
- Adults, €5.50; Students, €4.75; Family, €12.00
- Located on the main street in Kilbeggan town

At the Locke's Distillery Museum visitors can take a step back in time and visit the "oldest licensed pot still distillery in the world", established in 1757. Guided tours go through the old distillery buildings where most of the original machinery, which has been restored, can be seen working daily. Visitors can also learn about the lives and working conditions of the people who worked here. The exhibition houses many whiskey-related artefacts and has a children's play area.

Tullynally Castle Gardens

Castlepollard, Co Westmeath
Tel: 044-61159   Fax: 044-61856
www.tullynallycastle.com

- Open May 1 to August 31, 2.00 to 6.00
- Adults, €6.00; Children, €3.00; Family, €16.00
- Located two km from Castlepollard, on the Granard Road

Tullynally Castle gardens has over ten hectares of romantic woodland and walled gardens created over 300 years, and is set beside one of Ireland's largest castles to survive as a family home. There is a huge amount of space for families, and a specially designed Treasure Trail with attractions for children. These include fantastic carvings in roots and trees, a spooky grotto, a Chinese pagoda, two ornamental lakes with ducks and swans and a family of woolly llamas in the walled gardens.

Viking Tours

7 St Mary's Place, Athlone, Co Westmeath
Tel: 090-6473383   Fax: 090-6473392
vikingtours@ireland.com   www.iol.ie/wmeathtc/viking/

- Open May to September
- Fees vary depending on group size
- Sailings from The Strand Fishing Tackle Shop, Athlone Town Centre
- Caters for children's parties
- Caters for school groups/tours

The *Viking I* takes visitors back 1,200 years to when Viking war bands roamed and pillaged in these waters. Cruises are to Lough Ree and to the monastic site of Clonmacnoise. During the cruise to Lough Ree and its islands visitors listen to live commentary with tales of Viking treasure and of many battles fought. The ship's crew are dressed in Viking attire and passengers are invited to dress similarly for photos of themselves which are provided free of charge. There is a free Viking scroll for each child.

Ballyhack Castle

Ballyhack, Co Wexford
Tel: 051-389468
www.heritageireland.ie

- Contact castle for opening times
- Adults, €1.60; Children, €1.10; Family, €4.50
- Located in Ballyhack village off R733

Ballyhack Castle is located on a steep slope in a commanding position overlooking Waterford estuary. The castle, a large tower house, is thought to have been built c. 1450 by the Knights Hospitallers of St. John, one of the two great military orders founded at the beginning of the twelfth century at the time of the Crusades. *An OPW site.*

Berkeley Costume and Toy Museum

Berkeley Forest, New Ross, Co Wexford
Tel: 051-421361

- Open May to October, groups only
  by appointment
- Admission, €6.00
- Located 2.5 miles from New Ross
  on the Enniscorthy Road

The Berkeley Costume and Toy Museum consists of a private collection of costume and toys dating from 1750 to 1924. It is housed in the former drawing room and dining room of this late eighteenth-century house. The property formed the estate of the family of George Berkeley, the well-known eighteenth-century Irish philosopher. The exhibits include silk court dresses of an Irish provenance, eighteenth-century wooden dolls and a good cross-section of Victorian costumes and toys. There is also a handsome doll house, lavishly furnished. All tours are personally guided by the proprietor, Countess Ann Bernstorff. Catering can be organised for large groups and the gardens of the house are available for picnics.

Boolavogue — Fr Murphy Centre

Ferns, Co Wexford
Tel: 054-66898
bookings@boolavogue.info   www.boolavogue.info/home.html

- Open Sunday to Friday, 12.00 to 5.00;
  Saturdays by appointment only
- Contact the Centre for admission rates
- Located in Boolavogue, 16 km from Gorey
- Caters for school groups/tours

For most of the fourteen years that Fr. John Murphy was a curate in Boolavogue he lived with John O'Donohoe and his family in a house in Tomnaboley in Boolavogue. That house was destroyed in the rebellion and rebuilt afterwards. It was used until the late nineteenth century and then fell into disrepair. It was restored as part of the commemoration of the bicentennial of the 1798 Rebellion. It is situated in a restored farmyard which includes a cowhouse, pigsty, stable, dairy and labourers' lodge. The haggard contains a range of farm machinery, ploughs, harrows and sowers from the nineteenth and twentieth centuries.

Dunbrody Abbey Visitors Centre

Campile, Co Wexford
Tel: 051-388603
jfktrust@iol.ie   www.dunbrodyabbey.com

- Open from beginning of May to mid-September, 11.00 to 6.00
- Admission to Abbey: Adults, €2.00; Children, €1.00; Family, €5.00; separate admission to Maze, Castle and pitch and putt
- Located on the main road from New Ross to the Hook Peninsula
- Caters for school groups/tours

🍴 ♂♀

Dunbrody Abbey, founded in 1170, is one of the finest examples of a Cistercian monastery in Ireland. Dunbrody Abbey was founded on the instructions of Strongbow, by Herve de Montmorency (his uncle), after the Norman invasion of Ireland. It was completed circa 1220, but additions may have continued for some time. Next to the Abbey is Dunbrody Castle, and in the Castle garden is an intricate yew hedge maze made with 1,500 yew trees. It is one of only two full-size mazes in Ireland.

Dunbrody Emigrant Ship

JFK Trust, South Quay, New Ross, Co Wexford
Tel: 051-425239   Fax: 051-425240
jfktrust@iol.ie   www.dunbrody.com

HeritageISLAND
IRELAND'S VISITOR ATTRACTIONS

- Open April to September, 9.00 to 6.00; October to March, 10.00 to 5.00
- Adults, €7.00; Children, €4.00; Family, €18.00
- Located in New Ross on the main N25 route
- Caters for school groups/tours

🍴 ♿ ♂♀ 🎁

Visitors to New Ross will immediately be drawn to the magnificent sight of the masts and rigging of the historic emigrant ship *Dunbrody* towering over the quayside. *Dunbrody* is a full-scale replica of the original ship built in 1845 which carried thousands of emigrants from Ireland to North America over a period of 30 years. Visitors will experience the sights, smells and sounds of a tall ship crossing the ocean, as well as meeting the captain and crew, and encountering emigrants telling their stories. *Dunbrody* recalls the romantic age of sailing ships as well as giving a unique insight into an important period of Ireland's history.

Duncannon Fort Visitor Centre

Duncannon, New Ross, Co Wexford
Tel: 051-389454   Fax: 051-389454
duncannonfort@hotmail.com   www.thehook-wexford.com

- Open June to September, 10.00 to 5.30
- Adults, €5.00; Children, €3.00; Family, €12.00
- Located in Duncannon, south of New Ross
- Caters for school groups/tours

🍽 ♿ 🚻 🎒

Duncannon Fort is a star-shaped fortress on a strategically important promontory in Waterford harbour. Built in 1586 in the expectation of an attack by the Spanish Armada, the fort was subsequently refurbished and strengthened due to threats by Napoleon and Hitler. Today visitors can see the Comoradh Sundial, which acts as a permanent memorial to the events of 1798; a dry moat, whose inner walls are 30 feet high; a lighthouse built in 1774, and a spectacular view across the estuary to Co Waterford.

Ferns Castle

Ferns, Co Wexford
Tel: 056-24623
www.heritageireland.ie

- Contact Castle for opening times
- Adults, €1.60; Children, €1.00; Family, €4.50
- Located in centre of Ferns

🍽 🚻

The castle was built in the thirteenth century, possibly by William, Earl Marshall. Originally, the castle formed a square, with large corner towers. Only half of the castle now remains. The most complete tower contains a fine circular chapel, with carved ornament. The tower also has several original fireplaces and a vaulted basement. Archaeological excavations revealed a rock-cut ditch outside the castle walls. Ferns Castle is one of a number of historic sites in Ferns. Others include St Mary's, a twelfth-century Augustinian Priory; the remains of a thirteenth-century cathedral, part of which is incorporated into the present Church of Ireland Church; and St Peter's, a small nave and chancel church. *An OPW site.*

Forest Park Leisure Centre

Courtown, Gorey, Co Wexford
Tel: 053-9424849   Fax: 053-9424850
auracourtown@eircom.net   www.holohan.ie

- Open year round, 7.30 to 10.00, Monday and Wednesday; 9.00 to 10.00, Tuesday, Thursday and Friday; 10.00 to 7.00, Saturday and Sunday
- Peak season: Adults, €7.50; Children, €5.50; Family, €22.00.
- Located five miles from Gorey off the N11
- Caters for children's parties
- Caters for school groups/tours

The Forest Park Leisure Centre offers fun, fitness and health for the whole family. The centre includes three swimming pools, a toddlers' pool and a 65-metre water slide. Adults can relax with massage, beauty treatments, sauna, jacuzzi and steam room. The centre also offers children fun sessions in the water featuring "Harry the Hippo".

Hook Lighthouse

Hook Heritage Centre, Hook Head, Fethard-on-Sea, Co Wexford
Tel: 051-397055   Fax: 051-397056
thehook@eircom.net   www.thehook-wexford.com

- Open daily year round; guided tours every day from March to October; October to March at weekends only
- Adults, €5.50; Children, €3.00; Family, €15.00
- Hook Head is located in the SW corner of Co Wexford on the eastern boundary of Waterford Harbour
- Caters for school groups/tours

Hook Lighthouse is a unique example of an almost intact medieval lighthouse. It dates back to the early thirteenth century and was a major feat at the time of its construction. It has served sailors and shipping for 800 years and is thought to be one of the oldest operational lighthouses in the world. Visitors will enjoy a tour of the lighthouse with its fascinating history as well as spectacular views of the Hook Peninsula.

Irish Agricultural Museum

Johnstown Castle, Wexford
Tel: 053-42888   Fax: 091-42213

- Open all year, 9.00 to 5.00 (mainly)
- Adults, €6.00; Children/Students, €4.00; Family, €20.00
- Located four miles SW of Wexford Town
- Caters for school groups/tours

The Irish Agricultural Museum includes large, varied and fascinating exhibitions on Irish farming and country crafts. The setting is the 200-year-old farmyard on the grounds of Johnstown Castle (see separate listing on page 87) which has been sensitively restored. A mixture of traditional and high-tech methods are used to enliven the displays. The museum has been developed over a 30-year period to become a popular all-weather attraction in the south-east region.

Irish National Heritage Park

Ferrycarrig, Co Wexford
Tel: 053-20733   Fax: 053-20911
info@inhp.com   www.inhp.com

HeritageISLAND
IRELAND'S VISITOR ATTRACTIONS

- Open daily year round, 9.30 to 6.30 (times subject to seasonal change)
- Adults, €7.00; Children, €3.50; Family, €17.50
- Located off the main Rosslare road, N11
- Caters for children's parties
- Caters for school groups/tours
- Special programmes for children

The Irish National Heritage Park takes the visitor on an unexpected adventure through 9,000 years of Irish history. Through living history re-enactments, visitors can see where and how people lived, what they wore, what they ate, how they worshipped and buried their dead, from the coming of man to the island to the arrival of the Normans in the twelfth century. Guided tours can be geared towards children of all ages and workbooks are available for a small charge.

The John F. Kennedy Arboretum

New Ross, Co Wexford
Tel: 051-388171   Fax: 051-388172
www.heritageireland.ie

- Open daily May to August, 10.00 to 8.00; April and September, 10.00 to 6.30; October to March, 10.00 to 5.00
- Adults, €2.90; Children, €1.30; Family, €7.40
- Located 12 km south of New Ross off R733

Dedicated to the memory of President John Fitzgerald Kennedy, the Arboretum is a plant collection of international standing. It covers 252 hectares (623 acres) on the southern slopes and summit of Slieve Coillte. It contains 4,500 types of trees and shrubs from all temperate regions of the world, planted in botanical sequence. There are 200 forest plots grouped by continent. A road provides access to the summit at 271 metres from which there are panoramic views. A Visitor Centre houses exhibitions and an audio-visual show. *An OPW site.*

Johnstown Castle Gardens

Johnstown Castle Estate, Wexford
Tel: 053-42888   Fax: 053-42213

- Open all year, 9.00 to 5.00 (mainly). Closed for lunch off-season; closed weekends and bank holidays November to May
- Cost: €5.00 per car, including passengers
- Located four miles SW of Wexford Town
- Caters for school groups/tours

Johnstown Castle is surrounded by 50 acres of ornamental gardens, which include three lakes, a medieval tower house, walled gardens with hothouses and over 200 species of mature trees and shrubs. A car-free zone with many different walks, all on level ground, and a serviced picnic area are also on the grounds. Peacocks wander free. The Irish Agricultural Museum (see separate listing on page 86) is within the gardens.

National 1798 Centre

Millpark Road, Enniscorthy, Co Wexford
Tel: 054-37596   Fax: 054-37198
98com@iol.ie   www.iol.ie/~98com

- Open March to September, Monday to Friday, 9.30 to 6.00; weekends, 11.00 to 6.00; October to February, Monday to Friday, 9.30 to 4.00; closed weekends
- Adults, €6.00; Children, €4.00; Family, €16.00
- Located just off the N11 and N30 500 metres from Enniscorthy
- Caters for school groups/tours
- Special programmes for children

The Centre tells the epic and heroic tale of the 1798 Rebellion and its aftermath using the latest multimedia and interactive computers. A spectacular audio-visual presentation places the story in an international context and state-of-the-art exhibition techniques are used to give visitors a glimpse of our fascinating journey to modern democracy.

Ross Adventure Play Barn

Woodbine Business Park, New Ross, Co Wexford
Tel: 051-455817
rossadventureplaybarn@eircom.net   www.rossadventureplaybarn.com

- Open Monday to Saturday, 10.00 to 7.00; Sunday, 12.00 to 6.00
- Admission, €6.00 per child
- Located off the N25 ring road in New Ross
- Caters for children's parties
- Caters for school groups/tours
- Special programmes for children

Ross Adventure Play Barn provides a spacious 6,400 square foot soft play centre. Suitable for children up to ten years of age, the Centre is air-conditioned with a coffee shop, newspapers and a TV. CCTV is provided for security and safety, and there is a separate party area providing hot meals.

Quad Attack

Clonroche, Enniscorthy, Co Wexford
Tel: 053-9244660   Fax: 053-9244225
info@quadattack.ie   www.quadattack.ie

- Open seasonally
- Adult bikes, €38.00 for one hour, €28.00 for 45 minutes; Child bikes, €23.00 for one hour, €18.00 for 45 minutes; Adult bikes accompanying children, €33.00
- Located between Enniscorthy and New Ross on N30
- Caters for school groups/tours

♦ ♦

Quad Attack provides adventurous all-weather cross-country driving on quad bikes (ATVs) over a rugged 80-acre course. Children (from six up) usually start on the enclosed level track and then advance to some sections of the cross-country track where they can be accompanied by adults in the group. Helmets are provided and all tours are supervised. Also features newly installed indoor play centre including bouncy castle, sumo-wrestling, and bouncing bull. New at Quad Attack is the Crazy Corral. Test your skills on the Rodeo Bull, beat the bungee or burst, wrestle your opponent to the ground in a Sumo Suit.

Tintern Abbey

Saltmills, New Ross, Co Wexford
Tel: 051-562650
www.heritageireland.ie

- Open daily mid-June to late September, 9.30 to 6.30
- Adults, €2.10; Children, €1.10; Family, €5.80
- Located 16 km south of New Ross off R734

🍴 ♿ ♦ ♦

Tintern Abbey is a Cistercian abbey, founded c. 1200 by William, the Earl Marshall, and named after Tintern in Wales. The remains consist of nave, chancel, tower, chapel and cloister. It was partly converted into living quarters after 1541, and further adapted over the centuries. The Abbey was occupied by the Colclough family from the sixteenth century until the 1960s. *An OPW site.*

Wexford Arts Centre

Cornmarket, Wexford
Tel: 053-23764   Fax: 053-24544
wexfordartscentre@eircom.net   www.wexfordartscentre.ie

- Open Monday to Saturday, 10.00 to 6.00
- No entrance fee; different admissions for shows (children's admission usually 60 per cent of adult admission)
- Caters for school groups/tours
- Special programmes for children

♦♦

Wexford Arts Centre is open year round with activities in visual arts, theatre, music, literature and community arts. Visitors should contact the Centre for programme details or to receive the monthly newsletter. Typical children's events include art classes, exhibitions, puppet shows, plays by and for children, seasonal shows and school projects.

The Wexford Wildfowl Reserve

North Slob, Co Wexford
Tel: 053-23129   Fax: 053-24785
www.heritageireland.com

- Open daily April 16 to September 30, 9.00 to 6.00; October 1 to April 15, 10.00 to 5.00
- No entrance fee
- Located eight km NE from Wexford (signposted from Castlebridge Road)
- Caters for school groups/tours

♿ ♦♦

The Wexford Wildfowl Reserve, partly owned by BirdWatch Ireland, is situated on the North Slob which is internationally famous for wild geese that spend the winter months here. The first geese, Greylags from Iceland, came to the Slobs in 1898. Currently about 10,000 Greenland white-fronted geese spend the winter on the Wexford Slobs. The Visitor Centre has many interesting exhibitions and an audio-visual show. *An OPW site.*

Yola Farmstead

Tagoat, Rosslare Harbour, Co Wexford
Tel: 053-32610   Fax: 053-32612
wexgen@eircom.net

- Open daily May to October, 10.00 to 6.00 from March, April; November open Monday to Friday, 10.00 to 4.30
- Adults, €6.00; Children €4.50; Family, €15.00
- Located on the N25 between Rosslare Harbour and Tagoat
- Caters for school groups/tours

Yola Farmstead boasts some of the most beautiful and rare sights to be seen in the County of Wexford, from the Blacksmith's Olde Forge to St Helen's four-seater church. The wonderful Herbal Walk is another attraction that must be seen as well as the working Windmill, which is a beautiful copy of another windmill to be found in Le Harve, France. Visitors can find out how milk, cheese, and butter used to be made in The Dairy. Yola also includes a large number of beautiful and rare animals and fowl in the Animal's Corner and there is also a children's playground.

Arklow Maritime Museum

St Mary's Road, Arklow, Co Wicklow
Tel: 0402-32868

- Open Monday to Saturday, 10.00 to 5.00 (closed 1.00 to 2.00)
- Contact museum for admission fees
- Located in Arklow village, three-minute walk from Tourist Office
- Caters for school groups/tours

Arklow's maritime history stretches back centuries. In the ninth century the Vikings established the town and port on a permanent basis and the Normans consolidated its seafaring traditions. By the early twentieth century Arklow was Ireland's premier fishing port with a fleet of 80 schooners, brigs and brigantines. This proud tradition is reflected in the Arklow Maritime Museum's collection of painting, models, photographs, tools and equipment and can be viewed on the video "Eyes to the Sea". Also houses a model train exhibition.

Avondale House and Forest Park

Rathdrum, Co Wicklow
Tel: 0404-46111   Fax: 0404-46333
Jean.costelloe@coillte.ie   www.coillte.ie

HeritageISLAND
IRELAND'S VISITOR ATTRACTIONS

- Open daily from March 17 to October 31,
  11.00 to 6.00 (House closed Mondays
  March–April and September–October)
- Adults, €5.50; Family, €16.00
- Located one mile from Rathdrum on R752
- Caters for school groups/tours

A vondale House was the birthplace and home of Charles Stewart Parnell (1846–1891) one of the greatest political leaders of Irish history. It is set in a magnificent forest park of over 500 acres with tree trails and walks ranging in duration from one to five hours. The Georgian House, designed by James Wyatt and built in 1777, contains fine plasterwork and many original pieces of furniture. Other facilities include picnic areas, children's play area and Deer Pen containing a number of Sika Deer.

Clara Lara Fun Park

Vale of Clara, Rathdrum, Co Wicklow
Tel: 0404-46161
dayout@claralara.com

- Open May to first weekend of September, 10.30 to 6.00
- Admission €8.00 (under-fours no charge); additional
  charges for some activities, or unlimited extra rides for
  extra €8.00
- Located between Laragh and Rathdrum in Co Wicklow
- Caters for children's parties
- Caters for school groups/tours

C lara Lara Funpark is a unique outdoor adventure park for families and groups of children up to 12 years of age. Set in 50 acres astride the beautiful Avonmore River, attractions include boating, canoeing, water slides, junior go-carts, crazy golf, tarzan swings, tree houses, picnic areas and restaurant, barbecues and plenty more. Visitors are advised to bring old shoes and a change of clothes!!

Dwyer McAllister Cottage

Derrynamuck, Knockanarrigan, Co Wicklow
Tel: 0404-45325
www.heritageireland.ie

- Open daily mid-June to mid-September, 2.00 to 6.00
- No entrance fee
- Located nine km SW of Donard

🚻

The cottage nestles in the shade of Kaedeen mountain at the top of a grassy lane off the Donard to Rathdangan road in Co. Wicklow. It is a fine example of a traditional thatched cottage built with local stone and whitewashed inside and out. It was from this cottage, in the winter of 1799, that the famed rebel Michael Dwyer fought the encircling British groups and finally made good his escape over the snow-covered mountains. The cottage was later destroyed by fire and lay in ruins for almost 150 years. It was restored to its original form as a monument in the late 1940s and again extensively repaired and re-roofed in 1992. *An OPW site.*

Glendalough Visitor Centre

Bray, Co Wicklow
Tel: 0404-45325 Fax: 0404-45626
www.heritageireland.com

- Open daily mid-March to mid-October, 9.30 to 6.00; mid-October to mid-March, 9.30 to 5.00
- Adults, €2.90; Children, €1.30; Family, €7.40
- Located in Glendalough village

♿ 🚻

This early Christian monastic site was founded by St Kevin in the sixth century. Set in a glaciated valley with two lakes, the monastic remains include a superb round tower, stone churches and decorated crosses. The Visitor Centre has an interesting exhibition and an audio-visual show, "Ireland of the Monasteries". French, German, Spanish and Swedish guided tours are available all year by advance booking. *An OPW site.*

Glenroe Farm

Ballygannon, Kilcoole, Co Wicklow
Tel: 01-2872288   Fax: 01-2872298
mail@glenroefarm.com   www.glenroefarm.com

- Open April to August, 10.00 to 5.00 on
  weekdays, 10.00 to 6.00 on weekends
  (weekends only in March and September);
  open December for Santa visits
- Enquire about admission costs
- Located just off the N11 20 miles south of
  Dublin in Kilcoole
- Caters for children's parties
- Caters for school groups/tours

Situated in the picturesque village of Kilcoole, this family-run farm offers close and easy access to horses, deer, goats, sheep, pigs, ducks, geese, peacocks, rabbits, guinea pigs and chipmunks. There is also a Pet's Corner where children can find their favourite furry animals as well as an outdoor playground. The farm was one of the principal filming locations for 18 years for RTE's popular TV series *Glenroe*. Ideal venue for crèche, Montessori, school outings and summer camps.

Greenan Farm Museums and Maze

Ballinanty, Greenan, Rathdrum, Co Wicklow
Tel: 0404-46000   Fax: 0402-36308
will@greenanmaze.com   www.greenanmaze.com

- Open daily May to August, 10.00 to 6.00 (closed
  Mondays May to June); open Sundays only September to
  October
- Contact Greenan for admission fees
- Located six km from Rathdrum
- Caters for school groups/tours

Greenan Farm Museums and Maze is situated in midst of the Wicklow Mountains near the beautiful Glenmalure Valley. Among the many attractions are the Farm Museum, the Old Farmhouse Museum and the Bottle Museum — all of which provide an understanding of life on a traditional hill-farm — a challenging Maze and a Farm Walk where numerous wild and farm animals can be seen. Visitors will enjoy a fun-filled day incorporating heritage, education, nature and relaxation.

Kilmacurragh

Rathdrum, Co Wicklow
Tel: 01-8570909   Fax: 01-8570080
www.heritageireland.ie

- Open year round Monday to Saturday, 9.00 to 6.00; Sunday, 11.00 to 6.00
- No entrance fee
- Located five km south of Rathnew off N11

This arboretum is particularly famous for its conifers and calcifuges, planted during the nineteenth century by Thomas Acton in conjunction with David Moore and his son, Sir Frederick Moore, curators of the National Botanic Gardens in Glasnevin. It was a time of great botanical and geographical explorations with numerous species from around the world being brought back to Ireland through Glasnevin. There is limited access for visitors with disabilities. *An OPW site.*

Killruddery House and Gardens

Southern Cross, Bray, Co. Wicklow
Tel. 01 2863405 (Estate Office)   0404-46024 (Visitor and Event Manager)
info@killruddery.com   www.killruddery.com

HeritageISLAND
IRELAND'S VISITOR ATTRACTIONS

- House open May, June and September daily, 1.00 to 5.00; Gardens open daily, May to September, 1.00 to 5.00; April open weekends, 1.00 to 5.00
- House and Gardens, Adults, €8.00; Children, €3.00; Family, €18.00
- Located on Southern Cross Road off the N11 at Bray South
- Caters for school groups/tours

♦ ♦

Killruddery has been home to the Earls of Meath for nearly 400 years and is located just half an hour due south of Dublin. Because of the fine Elizabethan Revival architecture, historic seventeenth-century garden layout and magnificent Orangery, the House and Gardens are an invaluable resource to students of the decorative arts, classical sculpture and landscape design. The Angles, Long Ponds, Wilderness, Sylvan Theatre, Ornamental Dairy and Orangery are prominent features of this exceptional property.

National Sea Life Centre

Strand Road, Bray, Co. Wicklow
Tel. 01 2866939
slcbray@merlinentertainments.biz   www.sealife.ie

- Open May to September, daily, 10.00 to 6.00; rest of year, weekdays, 11.00 to 5.00; weekends, 11.00 to 6.00
- Adults, €9.75; students, €8.00; children 3-16, €6,95; Family, €31.00
- Located on the Strand Road in Bray
- Caters for school groups/tours

The National Sea Life Centre Bray invites visitors to enjoy a journey through the magical world of underwater wildlife . . . without getting wet! Featuring 24 spectacular displays, National Sea Life Centre Bray offers an unforgettable insight into the marvels of Ireland's freshwater and marine world, as well as the opportunity to view, at close quarters, creatures from all over the world. With over 70 different species on view, the visit culminates at our breathtaking ocean feature: Tropical Shark Lagoon (home to black tip reef sharks and leopard sharks).

Powerscourt House and Gardens

Powerscourt Estate, Enniskerry, Co Wicklow
Tel: 01-2046000   Fax: 01-2046900
www.powerscourt.ie

- House and Gardens open daily year round, 9.30 to 5.30
- Adults, €9.00; Children, €5.00; Children under five free
- Located 12 miles from Dublin off the N11

One of the world's great gardens, Powerscourt is situated in the foothills of the Wicklow Mountains. The garden was begun by Richard Wingfield in the 1740s and stretches out over 47 acres. It is a sublime blend of formal gardens, sweeping terraces and ornamental lakes together with secret hollows, rambling walks, walled gardens and over 200 variations of trees and shrubs. The eighteenth-century palladian house now incorporates an innovative shopping experience, terrace café, house exhibition and garden pavilion.

Russborough

Blessington, Co Wicklow
Tel: 045-865239   Fax: 045-865054
russborough@eircom.net

- Open daily May to September, 10.00 to 5.00; April and October, Sundays and Bank Holidays, 10.00 to 5.00
- Adults, €6.00; Students, €4.50; Children under 12, €3.00
- Located two miles south of Blessington

Russborough is the finest house in Ireland open to the public. It was built between 1740 and 1750 in the palladian style by Richard Castle (Cassells) with fine stucco ceilings by the Lafranchini brothers. Home of the internationally famous Beit Collection of paintings, it is beautifully maintained and lavishly furnished with fine displays of silver, porcelain, fine furniture, tapestries and carpets.

Wicklow's Historic Gaol

Kilmantin Hill, Wicklow Town, Co Wicklow
Tel: 0404-61599   Fax: 0404-61612
wccgaol@eircom.net   www.wicklowshistoricgaol.com

- Open daily March to September, 10.00 to 6.00; October, 10.00 to 5.00
- Adults, €6.80; Children, €3.95; Family, €18.20
- Located at the top of Wicklow Town, beside the Courthouse
- Caters for school groups/tours

Visitors to Wicklow's Historic Gaol can hear stories as told by the Gaoler, Richard Hoey, the nineteenth century Gaol Matron, Mary Morris, and the Ship's Captain, Luckyn Betts, as they take you on an unforgettable journey through Irish history. Wander through the cells, explore the recently re-opened Dungeon, meet the inmates and listen to their stories before you embark upon a journey to Botany Bay aboard the Hell Ship the *Hercules*.

Wicklow Mountains National Park

Education Centre, Upper Lake, Glendalough, Co Wicklow
Tel: 0404-45656   Fax: 0404-45710
wmnp@environ.ie   www.wicklownationalpark.ie

- Open Monday to Friday, 9.00 to 5.30
- No entrance fee
- Located off the Miner's Track, approximately 300 metres from the Upper Lake Car Park
- Caters for school groups/tours

The National Park, which covers much of upland Wicklow, contains an area of approximately 20,000 hectares (49,421 acres). This includes large areas of mountain blanket bogs, including the Lugnaquilla and Liffey Head Bog complexes and Glendalough Wood Nature Reserve. The National Park provides protection for the landscape and the wildlife, from rare orchids to the wild and beautiful Peregrine Falcon. The Education Centre provides a range of courses and tours for schoolchildren, students and other groups. These are related to nature conservation and the ecology of the National Park. *An OPW site.*

For the Kids in Munster

Aillwee Cave

Ballyvaughan, Co Clare
Tel: 065-7077067   Fax: 065-7077107
www.aillweecave.ie

- Open daily year round from 10.00 (closing times vary). December by appointment only.
- Adults, €10.00; Children, €5.00; Family, €25.00–€30.00
- Located five km south of Ballyvaughan
- Caters for school groups/tours
- Provides guided tours
- Special events: Easter egg hunt; Hallowe'en weekend; Santa's workshop

This stunning creation of nature, located in the Burren, was formed by the melt waters of a prehistoric ice age. The cave, carved out of limestone, cuts into the heart of the mountain. Visitors will see many splendid examples of formations in the Cave. Calcite formations resembling "Wasps' Nest", "Praying Hands" and "the Carrots" are to be seen as well as many others including a magnificent display of Straw Stalactites in the cascade chamber.

Bunratty Castle and Folk Park

Bunratty, Co Clare
Tel: 061-360788   Fax: 061-361020
www.shannonheritage.com

- Open daily year round, 9.30 to 5.30 (9.00 to 6.00 June to August); last admission to castle at 4.00
- Adults, €13.00; Children, €6.50; Family, €30.50
- Located eight miles north of Limerick
- Caters for school groups/tours

Bunratty Castle is the most complete and authentic medieval castle in Ireland. Built in 1425, and plundered on many occasions, it was authentically restored in 1954 to its former medieval splendour, with furnishings and tapestries which capture the mood of the times. Bunratty Folk Park recreates rural and urban life in nineteenth-century Ireland. Visitors can view farmhouses of various economic backgrounds, a watermill, church and village street. A traditional Irish evening is held in the Great Barn from April to October (reservations necessary).

The Burren Centre

Kilfenora, Co Clare
Tel: 065-7088030 Fax: 065-7088102
info@theburrencentre.ie   www.theburrencentre.ie

HeritageISLAND
IRELAND'S VISITOR ATTRACTIONS

- Open from mid-March to end May, 10.00 to 5.00; June to end August, 9.30 to 6.00; September to end October, 10.00 to 5.00
- Adults, €5.95, Children, €4.00; Family, €18.00
- Located on the Corofin to Lisdoonvara road in North Clare, ten minutes from Lisdoonvara
- Caters for school groups/tours

The visitor centre houses an exhibition and audio-visual display on the world-famous Burren Region. The exhibition has a state-of-the-art touch-screen map displaying flora, fauna, archaeology, geology and natural history of the Burren's rock terrain. Models of forts, castles and Stone Age life visually and simply recreate the splendour of the Burren's past.

The Burren Perfumery

Carron, Co Clare
Tel: 065-7089102   Fax: 065-7089200
burrenperfumery@eircom.net   www.burrenperfumery.com

- Open daily June to September, 9.00 to 7.00; October to May, 9.00 to 5.00. Closed Christmas week.
- Free entry
- Located one mile from Carron village, close to Ballyvaughan
- Caters for children's parties
- Has special programmes for children (by arrangement)

Ireland's oldest perfumery, deep in the unique Burren landscape, offers a herb garden with bird-watching area, a maze for children, and a kids' quiz to teach them about the wonders of the surrounding natural flora. There are demonstrations of the traditional perfume-extracting process, a short film on the region's history, and toys and books in the tearooms to keep the children entertained.

Clare Museum

Arthur's Row, Ennis, Co Clare
Tel: 065-6823382   Fax: 065-6842119
claremuseum@clarecoco.ie   www.clarelibrary.ie

- Open June to September, Monday to Saturday, 9.30 to 5.30; Sunday, 9.30 to 1.00; October to May, Tuesday to Saturday, 9.30 to 5.30
- Admission is free
- Located off O'Connell Square in Ennis town centre
- Caters for school groups/tours

Clare Museum's exhibition "The Riches of Clare: Its People, Place and Treasures," occupies two galleries and incorporates the traditional method of displaying original artefacts from the county with modern interpretive tools such as colourful display panels, audio visual and computer interactive presentations, models, some replicas and commissioned art pieces. The collection comprises a large display of archaeological material of local provenance on loan from the National Museum of Ireland and locally collected artefacts never seen before in public.

Craggaunowen — The Living Past

Kilmurry, near Quin, Co Clare
Tel: 061-367178   Fax: 061-361020
www.shannonheritage.com

- Open daily mid-April to September, 10.00 to 6.00 (group bookings on request in off season)
- Adults, €7.85; Children, €4.75; Family, €18.35–€19.40
- Located 12 miles SE of Ennis
- Caters for school groups/tours

Craggaunowen — The Living Past tells the story of the arrival of the Celts in Ireland — how they lived, farmed, hunted and died. Visitors can see a replica of a Crannóg (lake dwelling), Ring Fort and "An Iron Age Roadway". Craggaunowen Castle which was built around 1550 is also situated on the grounds. A major feature is the "Brendan Boat" built by Tim Severin who sailed from Ireland to Greenland, re-enacting the voyage of St Brendan, reputed to have discovered America centuries before Columbus. Children will see animals such as Soay sheep and wild boar which are actual species of the prehistoric era.

Dolphin Discovery

Kilrush Creek Marina, Kilrush, Co Clare
Tel: 065-9051327   Fax: 065-9051327
info@discoverdolphins.ie   www.discoverdolphins.ie

- Open daily from April to October (subject to demand and weather)
- Adults, €19.00; Children (under 16), €10.00
- Located at Kilrush Creek Marina, 43 kms from Ennis on N68
- Caters for school groups/tours

Dolphin Discovery offers daily trips to observe the resident group of bottlenose dolphins in their natural habitat in the Shannon estuary. Over 100 dolphins have been identified using the estuary at different times and calves are born each year between May and August. The Dolphin Discovery was purpose-built for dolphin watching and includes a hydrophone to allow visitors to listen to dolphins in their underwater acoustic world when conditions are suitable.

Dolphinwatch Carrigaholt

Carrigaholt, Co Clare
Tel: 065-9058156   Fax: 065-9058156
info@dolphinwatch.ie   www.dolphinwatch.ie

- Open daily April 1 to October 31 from 8.00 to 6.00
- Adults, €20.00; Children 3-16, €10.00; two and under, free; Group and charter rates available by request
- Located six miles SW of Kilkee
- Caters for children's parties
- Caters for school groups/tours

Dolphinwatch Carrigaholt offers visitors the unique opportunity of seeing bottlenose dolphins (Tursiops Truncatus) in their natural environment surrounded by breathtaking coastal beauty. At the mouth of the River Shannon between the Loop Head Peninsula (Co Clare) and Kerry Head (Co Kerry) lives a group of over 100 wild resident dolphins. They travel in small family groups within this area. The state-of-the-art nature tour vessel, built in 2000, offers the best possible comfort and safety for the entire family. The name of the vessel is *Draíocht*, meaning "magic" in the Irish language.

East Clare Heritage Centre

Tuamgraney, Co Clare
Tel: 061-921351
eastclareheritage@eircom.net   eastclareheritage.com

- Open year-round, Monday to Friday,
  10.00 to 5.00
- Adults, €4.00; Children, €2.00
- Located in St. Cronan's church, Tuamgraney
  village
- Caters for children's parties
- Caters for school groups/tours
- Provides guided tours

Built c. 930 AD, this church is the oldest in Ireland, England, Scotland and Wales that is still in use. Made of massive red sandstones, it has been described as the finest surviving specimen of the primitive type on the island. There is a permanent Brian Boru exhibition at the Centre, an audio-visual presentation, and a folk museum.

Glór – The Irish Music Centre

Friars Walk, Ennis, Co Clare
Tel: 065-6843103   Fax: 065-6845372
boxoffice@glor.ie   www.glor.ie

- Open year round 9.30 to 5.30 plus evening events
- Contact Centre for entrance fee details
- Located in Ennis town centre
- Caters for school groups/tours
- Special programmes for children

Glór – The Irish Music Centre is a performance space especially for Irish music, song and dance. As an arts centre, it also hosts theatre, ballet, film, visual arts and more. Some evening shows are suitable for children and there are also programmes specifically aimed at children from time to time. The annual St Patrick's Weekend Festival is programmed with children in mind with films, storytelling, face-painting and workshops.

Holy Island Tours

Scariff, Co Clare
Tel: 086-8749710
eastclareheritage@eircom.net   www.eastclareheritage.com

- Open daily April to September, 9.30 to 6.00
- Adults, €8.00; Children €4.00
- Located on Holy Island on Lough Derg
- Caters for children's parties
- Caters for school groups/tours
- Has special programmes for children
- Provides guided tours

Holy Island on Lough Derg and the river Shannon is one of the most famous monastic sites in Ireland. Its many attractions include a well-preserved Round Tower, the ruins of six churches, a Holy Well, a unique graveyard with slabs dating from the eight century, Bullaun Stones, a cell-like structure, which is one of the most extraordinary buildings in Ireland, and a "bargaining" stone where many a marriage was brokered. Their secluded position has enabled them to survive in a wonderful state of preservation.

Killaloe/Ballina Heritage Town

Brian Ború Heritage Centre, Killaloe, Co Clare
Tel: 061-376866   Fax: 061-361020
reservations@shannon-dev.oe   www.killaloe.ie

HeritageISLAND
IRELAND'S VISITOR ATTRACTIONS

- Open daily 10.00 to 6.00 (may be subject to change)
- Adults, €3.00; Children, €1.50; Family, €6.95 – €8.95
- Located in Killaloe Town Centre

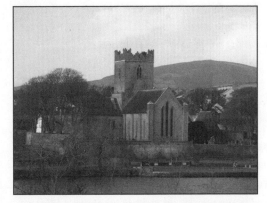

The majestically arched bridge, which joins these disparate twins, allows the River Shannon to pass gently seawards from the beautiful sylvan surrounding of Lower Lough Derg, where Ireland's most famous king, Brian Ború, held court at Kincora just one millennium ago. Killaloe, on the left bank, in County Clare is a network of charming narrow streets, flanked by old shops and houses, that climb up the steep hillside and look down over the thirteenth-century Cathedral. The buildings of Ballina, in North Tipperary, line the roadway that runs parallel to the river.

Kilrush Heritage Town

Kilrush Tourist Office, Kilrush, Co Clare
Tel: 065-9051577   Fax: 065-9052821
kilrush@clarecoco.ie   www.kilrush.ie

HeritageISLAND
IRELAND'S VISITOR ATTRACTIONS

- Open June to September, Monday to Saturday, 10.00 to 6.00; Sunday, 10.00 to 2.00
- No entrance fee
- Located in Kilrush Town Centre

Kilrush (Cill Ruis) is the primary business town for the west Clare peninsula. Its designation as a Heritage Town is in recognition of its legacy as a landlord estate town with a rich maritime and market tradition. Kilrush is situated on the mouth of the River Shannon, at the heart of one of Ireland's special interest marine tourism areas and surrounded by an unforgettable seascape featuring the islands of Scattery and Hogg.

Knappogue Castle

near Quin, Co Clare
Tel: 061-360788   Fax: 061-361020
reservations@shannondev.ie   www.shannonheritage.com

- Open daily April to early October, 9.30 to 5.30
- Adults, €6.25; Children, €3.15; Family, €14.15
- Located SW of Ennis near Quin
- Caters for school groups/tours

Knappogue Castle was built by Sean MacNamara in 1467. It is a sister to Bunratty Castle which was built by his father, Sioda, and is one of 42 or so such castles built in the area around the period. The MacNamara clan sold the castle to the Scotts in 1800 and in 1855 it was acquired by Lord Dunboyne. He made many additions to the Castle including the courtyard and clock tower as well as the walled garden. Today Medieval Castle Banquets are held in the Castle and it is also popular for gala events and private functions.

Lahinch Seaworld and Leisure Centre

The Promenade, Lahinch, Co Clare
Tel: 065-7081900   Fax: 065-7080901
lahinchseaworld@eircom.net   www.lahinchseaworld.com

- Open daily year round from 10.00
- Pool and aquarium: Adults, €13.00; Children, €9.00; Children 2-4, €6.00; Family, €38.00
- Located on the Promenade in Lahinch
- Caters for school groups/tours
- Caters for children's parties
- Special programmes for children

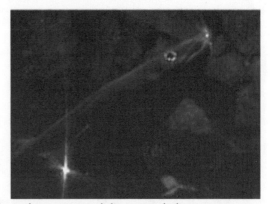

Visitors to Lahinch Seaworld can see and experience the amazing marine life on display in the aquarium, including native sharks, rays, conger eels and lobster. Other features include the Doolin Wave Tank, Touch Pools, an Ocean Tank and more. Facilities at the leisure centre include Spiral Tube Slide, Scramble Nets, Ball Pools, Pendulum Swings, Crawl Tubes, 25-metre pool, Kiddies Pool, Jacuzzi, Steam Room and Tanning Room.

Moher Hill Open Farm and Leisure Park

Cliffs of Moher Road, Liscannor, Co Clare
Tel: 065-7081071   Fax: 065-7086867
moherfarm@eircom.net   www.moherfarm.com

- Open daily, Easter to November, 10.00 to 6.00; Christmas Village open December 8-23
- €6.00 per person
- Located between Liscannor and the Cliffs of Moher
- Caters for children's parties
- Caters for school groups/tours
- Special programmes for children

Moher Hill Open Farm consists of ten acres of animal paddocks with Vietnamese pot belly pigs, goats, llama, donkeys, deer, ponies, sheep and many rare and domestic birds. Children are allowed to pet and feed the animals. There is also an indoor play area with a bouncy castle, sand diggers and go-karts, an under-fives play area, an outdoor play area and a nine-hole mini-golf course.

Scattery Island Centre

Merchant's Quay, Kilrush, Co Clare
Tel: 065-9052139
www.heritageireland.ie

- Open daily mid-June to mid-September, 10.00 to 6.00
- No entrance fee
- Located in village of Kilrush

♙ ♙

This Information Centre on the mainland interprets the island on which a monastery is sited. The monastery, consisting of a round tower and several churches, was founded by St Senan in the early part of the sixth century. His most famous pupil was St Ciaran of Clonmacnoise. A wonderful exhibition on the history of these monuments and on the wildlife of the area is housed in this Centre. Access for visitors with disabilities to ground floor. *An OPW site.*

West Clare Railway Company

Moyasta Junction, Kilrush, Co Clare
Tel: 065-9051284
info@westclarerailway.com   www.westclarerailway.com

- Open Monday to Saturday, from St Patrick's Day to end of October, 10.00 to 6.00; November to March, 10.00 to 5.00. Sundays, 12.00 to 5.00
- Adults, €7.00; Children, €3.50
- Located on the N67 between Kilrush and Kilkee
- Caters for children's parties
- Caters for school groups/tours

🍽 ♿ ♙♙ 🎁

West Clare Railway has now laid two miles of track and train rides are now available after 40 years. There are two "1892-style" carriages with a capacity of up to 80 passengers being pulled by a small diesel locomotive. Passengers get a four-mile round trip, a tour of the newly refurbished Railway Station and a chance to see some film footage from the 1950s when the train ran. The West Clare Railway was made famous by Percy French in his song "Are You Right There Michael".

Bantry House and Gardens

Bantry, Co Cork
Tel: 027-50047   Fax: 027-50795
info@bantryhouse.ie   www.bantryhouse.ie

- Open daily March 17 to October 31, 9.00 to 6.00 (House closed for West Cork Music Festival from June 27 to July 7)
- Adults, €10.00 (€5.00 for Gardens and 1796 Armada Exhibition Centre only); Children free when accompanied by parents
- Located just outside Bantry on the N71 road
- Cater for school groups/tours

B antry House, home to the White family since 1739, is one of the finest stately homes in Ireland and is in the process of being restored to its former elegance. The house contains Russian icons, eighteenth-century French, Flemish and Irish furniture and Gobelin tapestries. The 1796 Armada Exhibition Centre gives a history of the planned invasion by Theobald Wolfe Tone. The gardens, originally designed to be a reflection of all that was best in European design and style, are being restored. At the top of the 100 steps (the "Stairway to the Sky") is a beautiful view looking across Bantry Bay to the Cork/Kerry Mountains.

Barryscourt Castle

Carrigtwohill, Co Cork
Tel: 021-4882218
www.heritageireland.ie

- Open daily June to September, 10.00 to 6.00, October to May, 11.00 to 5.00
- Adults, €2.10; Children, €1.10; Family, €5.80
- Located off Cork-Youghal Road

B arryscourt Castle was the seat of the Barry family from the twelfth to the seventeenth centuries. The present castle is a fine example of a fifteenth-century tower house with sixteenth century additions and alterations. The bawn wall with three corner towers is largely intact. The ground floor of the keep houses an exhibition on the history of the Barrys and Barryscourt Castle. Managed in conjunction with Barryscourt Trust. *An OPW site.*

Blarney Castle

Blarney, Co Cork
Tel: 021-4385252   Fax: 021-4381518
info@blarneycastle.ie   www.blarneycastle.ie

- Open Monday to Saturday, June to August 9.00 to 7.00; May and September, 9.00 to 6.30; October to April, 9.00 to 6.00. Open Sundays, Summer, 9.30 to 5.30; Winter, 9.30 to sundown.
- Adults, €8.00; Children (0–14), €2.50; Family (two adults, two children), €18.00
- Located in Blarney, eight km from Cork City
- Caters for school groups/tours

Blarney Castle is one of Ireland's oldest and most historic castles, an ancient stronghold of the McCarthys, Lords of Muskerry, and one of the strongest fortresses in Munster. Blarney Castle is famous for its stone – The Stone of Eloquence – which is traditionally believed to have the power to bestow the gift of eloquence on all those who kiss it. In the grounds of the castle the Rock Close and gardens convey "druidic" charm and magical delights of centuries past.

Call of the Sea Visitor Centre

CoAction, North Road, Castletownbere, Co Cork
Tel: 027-70835   Fax: 027-71031
coactionbeara@eircom.net

- Open Monday to Friday, 10.00 to 5.00; weekends, 1.00 to 5.00
- Adults, €4.00; Children, €2.00; Family, €10.00
- Located in Castletownbere

The Call of the Sea Visitor Centre holds a wonderful treasure of local history which is of interest to children and adults. Using multi-sensory and interactive equipment, the story of the maritime history of the Beara region is brought to life. Visitors will hear Murty Og O'Sullivan, a well-known local pirateer, tell his life story, experience the sensation of being at sea during a thunderstorm, learn to use various pieces of marine equipment or take the place of a skipper of a fishing trawler on the high seas.

Cape Clear Museum and Archive

Cape Clear Island, Co Cork
Tel: 028-39119 or 021-4274110
www.placenames.ie/capeclear/museum.html

- Open daily 12.00 to 5.00 from June 1 to August 31 and from September to May by arrangement
- Admission fee, €4.00
- Cape Clear Island is located ten km southwest of Baltimore. Ferry service from Baltimore and Schull.

Cape Clear Museum is housed in a restored old schoolhouse and contains several hundred artefacts of island maritime and folklife interest. There are, to date, 196 framed exhibition panels in the collection which deal with fourteen different themes of island heritage. Cape Clear Island Archive is a comprehensive collection of baptism, marriage and burial records, headstone inscriptions, school rolls, census returns, maps, folklore, placename and genealogical archive. Also included is a compilation of some 2,200 photographs of island life which are individually catalogued in various themes.

Charles Fort National Monument

Summercove, Kinsale, Co Cork
Tel: 021-4772263   Fax 021-4774347
www.heritageireland.ie

- Open daily mid-March to October, 10.00 to 6.00; November to mid-March, 10.00 to 5.00
- Adults, €3.70; Students, €1.30; Family, €8.70
- Located three km from Kinsale off R600
- Caters for school groups/tours

Charles Fort is one of the largest military forts in Ireland and has been associated with some of the most momentous events in Irish history. The main exhibition centre includes audio-visual displays and interactive exhibits. Children in particular enjoy the touch-screen displays where they can "build" their own fort. Worksheets are provided for school groups suitable for nine- to twelve-year-olds. As Charles Fort is a military fortification, there are hazards such as unprotected edges and uneven ground and children need to be accompanied by adults and be sure to observe the warning signs. *An OPW site.*

Cobh Heritage Town

Cobh Heritage Centre, Railway Station, Cobh, Co Cork
Tel: 021-4813591   Fax: 021-4813595
info@cobhheritage.com   www.cobhheritage.com

- Open May to October, 9.30 to 6.00; November to April, 9.30 to 5.00
- Adults, €6.00; Children, €3.50; Family, €16.50
- Located off the N25 in Cobh
- Caters for school groups/tours
- Special programmes for children

🍽 ♿ 🚻 🎁

Cobh is situated on the southern shore of the Great Island in one of the world's finest natural harbours. Between 1848 and 1950, over six million adults and children emigrated from Ireland – over 2.5 million from Cobh, making it the single most important port of emigration in the country. Cobh was the last port of call for the ill-fated *Titanic*. Later the steamers and ocean liners continued carrying the Irish to new lives and new lands.

Cobh Museum

High Road, Cobh, Co Cork
Tel: 021-4814240
cobhmuseum@eircom.net   www.cobhmuseum.com

HeritageISLAND
IRELAND'S VISITOR ATTRACTIONS

- Open Easter to October, 11.00 to 1.00 and 2.00 to 5.00; Sunday, 3.00 to 6.00.
- Adults, €1.50; Family, €3.75
- Located in the former Presbyterian church, known as Scots Church, in Cobh
- Caters for school groups/tours

🚻 🎁

The displays in the museum reflect the maritime and cultural history of the town. The Great Island on which Cobh stands is the largest island in Cork Harbour. Cobh has had other names: Cove ("The Cove of Cork"), Queenstown (after the visit of Queen Victoria in 1849). Highlights at the museum include the History of Spike Island, Secrets of Cork Harbour, Mementoes of a Victorian Lady, *Lusitania* memorabilia, paintings, watercolours, photographs, sporting heroes of Cobh, shipping pilots of Cork Harbour and models of local ships.

Cork City Gaol

Convent Avenue, Sunday's Well, Cork
tel: 021-4305022   Fax: 021-4307230
corkgaol@indigo.ie   www.corkcitygaol.com

- Open daily March to October, 9.30 to 6.00; November to February, 10.00 to 5.00
- Adults, €6.00; Children, €3.50; Family (two adults, four children), €18.00
- Located two km from Patrick Street in Cork City
- Caters for school groups/tours

Cork City Gaol, located in a magnificent castle-like building — a former prison — is now a unique attraction for all the family. The atmosphere created by the life-size wax figures, exhibitions and sound effects provides visitors with an unforgettable experience. The focus of the exhibition is on the stories of ordinary men, women and children who were incarcerated, mainly for crimes we would not consider serious. Inside the Gaol is a separate exhibition, the "Radio Museum Experience", including the RTE museum collection.

Crawford Municipal Art Gallery

Emmet Place, Cork   Tel: 021-4273377   Fax: 021-4805043
crawfordgallery@eircom.net   www.crawfordartgallery.com

- Open year round, Monday to Saturday, 10.00 to 5.00
- No entrance fee
- Located in the city centre, near the Opera House
- Caters for school groups/tours
- Special educational programmes for children

Under the umbrella of the Irish Department of Education, the Crawford Municipal Art Gallery is a key educational and heritage resource for the city of Cork through the development of its permanent collection and temporary exhibition programme, as well as through lectures, musical concerts and, above all, an exciting and challenging programme of exhibitions accompanied by guided school tours and children's workshops.

Desmond Castle (French Prison)

Cork Street, Kinsale, Co Cork
Tel: 021-4774855   Fax: 021-4774855
www.heritageireland.ie

- Open daily mid-April to October, 10.00 to 6.00
- Adults, €2.90; Children, €1.30; Family, €7.40
- Located 600 metres from Guard Well along Cork Street

Built as a custom house by the Earl of Desmond c. AD 1500, Desmond Castle has a colourful history, ranging from Spanish occupation in 1601 to use as a prison for captured American sailors during the American War of Independence. It is known locally as "The French Prison" after a tragic fire in which 54 prisoners, mainly French seamen, died in 1747. The International Museum of Wine opened in Desmond Castle in 1997. It features an exhibition which documents the intriguing story of Ireland's wine links with Europe and the wider world from the early modern period to the present day. *An OPW site.*

Doneraile Wildlife Park

Doneraile, Co Cork
Tel: 022-24244
www.heritageireland.ie

- Open mid-April to October, Monday to Friday, 8.00 to 10.30, Saturday, 10.00 to 8.30; Sunday and Bank Holidays, 11.00 to 7.00. Open November to mid-April, Monday to Friday, 8.00 to 4.30; Saturday, Sunday and Bank Holidays, 10.00 to 4.30
- Adults, €1.60; Children, €1.00; Family, €4.50
- Located on Turpike Road north of Doneraile town

The park comprises approximately 166 hectares and is an outstanding example of an eighteenth-century landscaped park in the "Capability Brown" style. Mature groves of deciduous trees, several restored water features and a number of deer herds can be viewed along the many pathways within the park. Doneraile Court, the former residence of the Saint Leger Family, is situated within the Park. The pathways are generally accessible for visitors with disabilities. *An OPW site.*

The Donkey Sanctuary

Knockardbane, Liscarroll, Mallow, Co Cork
Tel: 022-48398   Fax: 022-48489
donkey@indigo.ie   www.thedonkeysanctuary.ie

- Open Monday to Friday, 9.00 to 4.30, weekends and bank holidays, 10.00 to 5.00
- No entrance fee
- Located one km from Liscarroll
- Caters for school groups/tours

Set in serene and relaxed surroundings in Co Cork, the Donkey Sanctuary has taken in over 2,000 donkeys from all parts of Ireland. Visitors are free to spend as much time as they wish, meeting the donkeys who adore receiving lots of fuss and attention. There are donkeys of all ages at the Sanctuary including those who have recently been taken into care who require ongoing veterinary attention. There is an Information Centre with visual displays, leaflets and additional information.

Fota House and Gardens

Fota Island, Carrigtwohill, Co Cork
Tel: 021-4815543   Fax: 021-4815541
info@fotahouse.com   www.fotahouse.com

HeritageISLAND
IRELAND'S VISITOR ATTRACTIONS

- Open daily April 1 to September 30, 10.00 to 5.00; October 1 to March 31, 11.00 to 4.00
- Adults, €5.50; Children, €2.20; Family, €13.00
- Located just off main Cork-Waterford Road
- Caters for school groups/tours

Fota Island comprises 316 hectares in area and lies approximately 12km east of Cork City. Fota House was the home of the Smith-Barry family from the mid-eighteenth century up until 1975. The house was designed by the famous Morrison architects and the arboretum and gardens are of international repute for their collection of rare and tender trees and shrubs. The detailed stories of Fota House are presented in a series of multi-media programmes, accessible on screens located around the house.

Fota Wildlife Park

Carrigtwohill, Co Cork
Tel: 021-4812678   Fax: 021-4812744
info@fotawildlife.ie   www.fotawildlife.ie

- Open daily mid-March to October 31, 10.00 to 5.00 (last admission); Sunday 11.00 to 5.00. Open November to mid-March, Saturday, 10.00 to 5.00, Sunday, 11.00 to 5.00
- Adults, €11.50; Children, €7.00 (no charge under two); Family and group rates available
- Located ten miles from Cork off the N25
- Caters for school groups/tours
- Special programmes for children

One of the most progressive wildlife parks in Europe, Fota has more than 90 species in open, natural surroundings. The animals are not restrained by cages or obvious barriers, yet visitors walk through the park in complete safety. Giraffes, zebras, ostrich and antelope roam together in 40 acres of grassland. Monkeys swing through the trees while kangaroos, macaws, lemurs and other species have complete freedom of the park. Facilities include playgrounds and a tour train.

Fox's Lane Folk Museum

Fox's Lane, Youghal, Co Cork
Tel: 024-91145

- Open during tourist season, Tuesday to Saturday, 10.00 to 6.00 (closed 1.00 to 2.00)
- Contact museum for admission fees
- Located in town centre near tourist office
- Caters for school groups/tours

Fox's Lane Folk Museum displays some 600 domestic gadgets and appliances which were used within the home from the 1850s to the 1950s. Visitors will see manually operated vacuum cleaners and washing machines, selections of early gramophones, sewing machines, telephones, typewriters and more. There is a wide selection of food preparation and cooking equipment including some unusual items like a cucumber straightener, egg topper, wasp trap and moustache cup. A questionnaire is available for children to keep a written record of the museum visit.

Keeping Kids Active in Sport

Sean Connor

"This is an island age — a hundred years ago you had to depend on other people . . . no one had TVs, or DVDs or videos or home espresso makers. As a matter of fact, they didn't have anything cool" (monologue by Hugh Grant in *About a Boy*).

This quote represents the key problems facing parents who would like their children to be physically active. Kids now have many choices as is particularly evidenced in this publication. They may like sport or physical activity but may choose to do other things like working or drinking or playing computer games. The biggest competition now to physical activity is home-based activity, often referred to as "cocooning". As our society continues to become increasingly wealthy, one effect of this is a corresponding increase in cocooning. The norm is that kids now have their own rooms with their own television and stereo. A mobile phone is a must as is an iPod. Increasingly, children are living an adult-like lifestyle at younger ages.

There are a number of other factors that are making it more difficult to keep children active. Roads are becoming busier each year and parents often don't feel it is safe for their children to walk or cycle to school. Similarly, it is often felt that it is not safe for children to play on the streets. More and more children are in childcare and this may affect activity levels. Time is taken up dropping and picking up children and the carers are often less likely to let children play outside than are parents. Insurance and other regulations are causing havoc in relation to play. A large number of primary schools now even ban children from running outside of PE times. It would seem a ridiculous situation to ban what is a natural activity for any child.

The liability issue is also a major factor in restricting the numbers who are willing to volunteer. The Code of Ethics and the scandals in relation to childhood sex abuse have meant there are now a plethora of regulations to be followed. Volunteers often don't mind giving up their time but increasing paper work is a major turn-off. The PE situation in primary schools is particularly poor, especially in comparison to other western democracies. There is a dearth of facilities, a lack of time in which to deliver a PE programme and a large number of primary teachers who don't feel competent to teach PE. Other constraints to participation include, in particular, the increasing prevalence of asthma, which now affects one in seven children. Similarly, childhood obesity is increasing significantly as we mimic the lifestyle of our US counterparts.

There have, however, been a number of initiatives recently to counteract the lack of sports in primary school. Firstly, a new PE curriculum for primary school has been developed which will have interesting possibilities if it is implemented. Secondly, the Irish Sports Council has invested in and supported a Buntús school sports programme. This programme acknowledges the real problems faced in primary schools and provides training and equipment for schools and teachers. The third initiative has been the direct links that have been established between schools and the national governing bodies of sport. The provision of coaches to schools by NGBs has helped to counteract the decline of volunteers. This is usually at no cost to the school as the governing bodies provide their development officers free of charge.

As the child enters secondary school, there is often an increase in activity levels. The adolescent may have PE for the first time and it is likely that the secondary school will have a greater variety of activities on offer than the primary school. At present, the level of provision of sport for able sportspeople in Irish secondary schools is good. The top athletes will have the chance to play on multiple school teams and also on local club teams. In contrast, the provision levels for the silent majority are usually very poor: 80 per cent of Leaving Cert students have 40 minutes or less of PE each week in schools.

Similarly, there is a remarkable over-emphasis on team games in schools: 90 per cent of PE classes are devoted to team games. For those students who would prefer individual sports like badminton, tennis, horse riding, etc, their needs are not generally being considered in Irish secondary schools.

As they pass through the adolescent years their interests change. At around 14 they become more focused on casual activities. This is where structured groups and clubs experience significant levels of dropping out by teenagers. At this stage of their lives teenagers like to hang out with their peers. Few agencies in Ireland accept this transition and it is often felt that teenagers are one of the most marginalised groups in Irish society. They get blamed for many of the ills yet seldom have their needs met or even considered. Residents associations and City and County Councils have landscaped green areas to prevent youths congregating. Teenagers are often moved on from shopping centres. Popular hanging-out areas like skateboard parks have either not been provided or are closed, with insurance usually being cited as the reason.

The following are some suggestions to help keep children more active. Where possible let them walk or cycle to school. This alone will often be enough to keep children healthy. Put pressure on schools to provide more facilities and time to sporting activities. Examine programmes that exist in secondary schools and particularly look at how the school caters for non-elite athletes. Programmes that focus on individual activities are particularly successful at keeping girls active. Allow children to try casual activities as they go through adolescence. This experimentation is part of normal childhood development. Resist the temptation to take away hanging-out areas in estates. This has led to underground and deviant behaviour and it is much better practice for adolescents to be hanging out in public areas. Like a child running in a primary school, this is a natural and normal activity.

Sean Connor lectures at Water ford Institute of Technology and is the author of Youth Sport in Ireland: The Sporting, Leisure and Lifestyle Patterns of Irish Adolescents.

Glengarriff Bamboo Park

Glengarriff, Co Cork
Tel: 027-63570   Fax: 027-63255
bambooparkltd@eircom.net   www.bamboo-park.com

- Open daily year round, 9.30 to 7.00
- Adults, €5.00; Students, €3.00; Children, free; dogs welcome!
- Located in Glengarriff

Visitors to one of the south west's most exotic gardens will see 30 different species of bamboo, 12 different species of palm trees, superb coastal woodland walks and unique views of Glengarriff Harbour. Most of the bamboo on view are giant bamboo which will eventually grow to 10 metres or more. Visitors can also see the tree ferns, probably the oldest plants in the world.

Ilnacullin (Garinish Island)

Glengariff, Bantry, Co Cork
Tel: 027-63040   Fax: 027-63149
www.heritageireland.ie

- Open May to September, Monday to Saturday 9.30 to 6.00 (10.00 in May, June and September), Sunday 11.00 to 6.30; March and October, Monday to Saturday, 10.00 to 4.30; Sunday, 1.00 to 5.00
- Adults, €3.70; Children, €1.30; Family, €8.70
- Located by 1.5 km boat ride from Glengariff

Located in the sheltered harbour of Glengariff in Bantry Bay, Ilnacullin is a small island of 15 hectares (37 acres) known to horticulturists and lovers of trees and shrubs all around the world as an island garden of rare beauty. The gardens of Ilnacullin owe their existence to the creative partnership, some 80 years ago, of Annan Bryce, then owner of the island, and Harold Peto, architect and garden designer. Please note that the boat operators impose a separate charge in respect of the boat journey to and from the island. Limited access for visitors with disabilities. *An OPW site.*

Kinsale Heritage Town

Kinsale Museum, Market Square, Kinsale, Co Cork
Tel: 021-4777930   Fax: 021-4777929
www.kinsale.ie

- Open June to October, Wednesday to Saturday, 10.30 to 5.30; Sunday, 2.00 to 5.00; November to May, Wednesday to Sunday, Wednesday to Saturday, 10.30 to 2.00, Sunday, 2.00 to 5.00
- Adults, €2.50; Students, €1.50; Children (accompanied), free
- Located in Kinsale town centre

For centuries, Kinsale has been a haven from the sea for travellers and traders alike. Their influence has made Kinsale the most cosmopolitan and charming of ports in Ireland. But where Britons, Spaniards and Irish once fought, yachts now disgorge their sailors to sample "fruits de mer" in the old world atmosphere of Ireland's Gourmet Capital. Sample the history of the "Wine Geese" in Ireland's only International Wine Museum in Desmond Castle and the history and crafts of Kinsale in the historic Courthouse. Visit Charles Fort and twelfth century St Multose Church or The Courthouse, which houses the Regional Museum.

Michael Collins Centre

Castleview, Clonakilty, Co Cork
Tel: 023-46107   Fax: 023-46107
info@michaelcollinscentre.com   www.michaelcollinscentre.com

- Open daily June to September
- Adults, €4.00; Children, free
- Located in Castleview, NE of Clonakilty

Visitors at the Michael Collins Centre can watch a 20-minute audio-visual which explores the Big Fella's childhood, his family history, his school days and the important Collins' sites around Clonakilty. A guide then continues the presentation, using slides, large photographs or film clips, and the visitor is taken through the 1916 rebellion, War of Independence, Treaty talks and the Civil War. The tragic death of Michael Collins at Béal Na Bláth and his legacy are also discussed. The presentation ends with a guided tour of the ambush trail, a life-size replica of an ambush site complete with Crossley Tender and replica of Michael Collins' famous Rolls Royce armoured car, "Sliabh Na mBan".

Millstreet Country Park

Millstreet, Co Cork
Tel: 029-70810   Fax: 029-70899
info@millstreetcountrypark.com   www.millstreetcountrypark.com

- Open daily St Patrick's Day to October 31, 10.00 to 7.00
- €15.00 per car; other group rates available
- Located on Mallow side of Millstreet village
- Special programmes for children

Millstreet Country Park, set on 203 hectares, is an environmental and nature park on the slopes of Musheramore mountain in North Cork. Visitors marvel at its expanse and attention to detail from colourful arboretum, deeply scented gardens, picturesque views and rushing waaterfalls to the Stone Circles, Crannóg and Fullacht Fiadh. The park is home to many species of birds and wild animals from the Red Deer to Wild Brown Trout to the Kingfisher. Children can use touch-screen computers in the Field Studies Laboratory to discover some of the wonders of nature.

Mizen Head Visitor Centre

Goleen, West Cork
Tel: 028-35115   Fax: 028-35422
info@mizenhead.net   www.mizenhead.net

HeritageISLAND
IRELAND'S VISITOR ATTRACTIONS

- Open daily June to September, 10.00 to 6.00; mid-March to May and October, 10.30 to 5.00; mid-November to March, weekends, 11.00 to 4.00
- Adults, €6.00; Children under 12, €3.50; Children under five, free; Family, €18.00
- Located at Ireland's most southwesterly point
- Caters for children's parties
- Caters for school groups/tours

An award-winning maritime museum and heritage attraction, this authentic all-weather experience is a must-see with its spectacular location on high cliffs with swirling Atlantic Ocean tides. From the car park and Visitor Centre, the Signal Station is a ten-minute walk along the path, down the 99 steps and across the Arched Bridge, the Mizen is famous for its wildflowers and sightings of wildlife, dolphins, whales, seals, gannets and choughs. Visitors can see displays of the building of the Fastnet Lighthouse, the keepers' kitchen and bedroom, sea life and underwater wrecks, the Engine Room and much more.

Old Midleton Distillery

Midleton, Co Cork
Tel: 021-4613594   Fax: 021-4613704
www.whiskeytours.ie

HeritageISLAND
IRELAND'S VISITOR ATTRACTIONS

- Open daily, 10.00 to 6.00
- Adults, €8.50. Children, €4.00
- Located in Midleton town

A tour of the Old Midleton Distillery is a journey through the story of Irish whiskey by means of an audio-visual presentation. Follow the old distillery trail through mills, maltings, corn stores, stillhouse, warehouses and kilns; some of these buildings date back to 1795. View the largest pot still in the world prior to sampling the internationally renowned Jameson Whiskey in the bar (minerals for children). You may even have the opportunity of becoming a qualified Irish whiskey taster with the presentation of a certificate before browsing in the exclusive Jameson merchandise outlet and craft shops or relaxing in the elegant restaurant on site.

Perks Fun Fair and East Cork Superbowl

Seafield Business Centre, Youghal, Co Cork
Tel: 024-92438   Fax: 024-93523
perkie@iol.ie   www.perksfunfair.com

- Open daily (telephone for times)
- No admission fee; prices for activities vary
- Located 26 miles from Cork city on N25 Cork to Waterford road
- Caters for children's parties
- Caters for school groups/tours

Perks Fun Fair is a large indoor fun fair with a Ghost Train, Kiddie Rides and free Crazy Mirrors. There is also an adventure play centre called "Captain Blackbeard's" based on a pirate theme with slides, rope climbing and more. The ten-pin bowling alley is fully computerised with automatic scoring. Also featured is the Megazone Lazer Tag Arena, a high-tech live action lazer game.

Prince August – Toy Soldier Factory

Kilnamartyra, Macroom, Co Cork
Tel: 026-40222   Fax: 026-40004
www.princeaugust.ie

- Open year round, Monday to Friday, 9.00 to 5.00
- No entrance fee
- Located two km off the N22, six km NW of Macroom

At the Prince August – Toy Soldier Factory visitors can see hundreds of highly collectible military figures, chess sets and historical figures crafted and painted by local specialists. Tolkien enthusiasts will enjoy the largest collection of Mithril Figures available in the world, depicting characters from *The Lord of the Rings* and *The Hobbit*. Also available are many dramatic dragons and spiders which have captured the imagination of so many readers.

Skibbereen Heritage Centre

Old Gasworks Building, Upper Bridge Street, Skibbereen, Co Cork
Tel: 028-40900   Fax: 028-40957
info@skibbheritage.com   www.skibbheritage.com   HeritageISLAND
IRELAND'S VISITOR ATTRACTIONS

- Open daily from June to mid-September, 10.00 to 6.00; mid-March to June and mid-September to October 31, open Tuesday to Saturday, 10.00 to 6.00
- Adults, €5.00; Children, €3.00; Family, €12.00
- Caters for school groups/tours
- Special programmes for children

Skibbereen Heritage Centre features the Great Famine Commemoration Exhibition which uses the latest multimedia technology to bring this period of Irish history to life. Visitors can also take a historical walking tour of the town. The Lough Hyne Visitor Centre offers a fascinating audio and visual insight into Ireland's first Marine Nature Reserve. Also featured is a salt water aquarium with species found in the lake. All situated in a beautifully restored historic riverside building with features on the Old Gasworks and its history.

West Cork Model Railway Village

"The Station", Inchydoney Road, Clonakilty, Co Cork
Tel: 023-33224
modelvillage@eircom.net   www.clonakilty.ie

- Open daily 11.00 to 5.00 (extended hours in summer)
- Admission: Adults, €6.50; Children, €4.00; under fives, €2.00. Train rides: Adults, €10.00; Children €6.00; Under-fives, €3.00
- Located in Clonakilty village

Visitors to the West Cork Model Railway Village can experience the sights and sounds of life in West Cork during the 1940s, enhanced by the miniature working railway which depicts the long-closed West Cork Railway. The towns of Clonakilty, Kinsale, Bandon and Dunmanaway are reconstructed in miniature on a scale of 1:24. New attractions added every year.

Youghal Heritage Centre

Market Square, Youghal, Co Cork
Tel: 024-20170   Fax: 024-20171
youghaltourism@eircom.net   www.youghalchamber.ie

HeritageISLAND
IRELAND'S VISITOR ATTRACTIONS

- Open April to October, Monday to Friday, 9.00 to 5.30; weekends, 9.30 to 5.00; rest of year enquire at 024-92447
- Entrance is free
- Located in Market Square, Youghal
- Caters for school groups/tours

Youghal Heritage Centre allows visitors to explore the history of the fascinating harbour town of Youghal. They learn about its medieval walls, links with Elizabethan adventurer Sir Walter Raleigh and with Richard Boyle, first Earl of Cork. Dramatic images and fine models are some of the techniques used to bring Youghal's history to life. Walking tours with group rates are available.

Adopt a Sheep

Kissane Sheep Farm, Moll's Gap, Kenmare, Co Kerry
Tel 064-34791
Adoptasheep@eircom.net   www.Adopt-a-Sheep.ie

- Open daily from April to October, 10.00 to 5.00
- Adults, €6.00; Children (under 11), €3.00; Family, €15.00 (no charge for Adoptive Parents)
- Located on the Ring of Kerry (N71) near Moll's Gap between Kenmare and Killarney
- Caters for children's parties
- Caters for school groups/tours
- Special programmes for children

On Kissane Sheep Farm you can experience the heritage of a working sheep farm with approx. 1,000 mountain sheep and hundreds of lambs in spring and summer. Visitors can meet the farmer, enjoy a sheepdog demonstration, see sheep being sheared (in shearing season) and do one of the three marked mountain walks. Especially for children there is an educational puzzle walk and an adventurous treasure trail on the farm. They can also help feeding the pet lambs with a bottle. On Kissane Sheep Farm you can adopt a sheep. In doing so you help to preserve the Irish heritage of sheep in the mountains.

Aqua Dome

Tralee, Co Kerry
Tel: 066-7128899   Fax: 066-7129130
aquadome@eircom.net   www.discoverkerry.com/aquadome

- Open Monday, Wednesday and Friday 10.00 to 10.00; Tuesday and Thursday 12.00 to 10.00; Weekends, 11.00 to 8.00
- Adults, €12.00; Children, €10.00; under 2s free; Family discounts available
- Located in Tralee (follow signs to Dingle)
- Caters for children's parties
- Caters for school groups/tours

Aqua Dome is Ireland's largest waterworld with features that include Sky High Water Slides, Falling Rapids, Wave Pool, Gushers and Geysers, Whirl Pools, Kiddies Pools and Slides; Water Cannons and a Medieval Castle. Located next to the Aqua Dome is Aqua Golf, an 18-hole miniature golf course.

Ardfert Cathedral

Ballyheigue Road, Ardfert, Co Kerry
Tel: 066-7134711
www.heritageireland.ie

- Open daily May to September, 9.30 to 6.30
- Adults, €2.10; Children, €1.10; Family, €5.80
- Located 10 km from Tralee on the R551
♿

A monastery was founded here by St. Brendan "The Navigator" in the sixth century. There are three medieval churches, an ogham stone and a number of early Christian and medieval grave slabs on the site today. The earliest building is the cathedral which dates from the twelfth to seventeenth centuries. It has a fine Romanesque west doorway, a magnificent thirteenth-century east window and a spectacular row of nine lancets in the south wall. One of the two smaller churches is a fine example of late Romanesque and the other is a plain fifteenth-century structure with an interesting carving of a wyvern on one of the windows. Access for people with disabilities to exhibition area and viewing point. *An OPW site.*

Burke's Activity Centre

Rossbeigh Beach, Glenbeigh, Co Kerry
Tel: 066-9768872   Fax: 066-9768872

- Open daily April 1 to November 1
- Entrance fee: €6.00 per person
- Located on the Ring of Kerry, 20 minutes from Killarney
- Caters for children's parties
- Caters for school groups/tours
- Special programmes for children

🍽 ♿ 🚻 🎁

B urke's Activity Centre is a working farm with a difference. Open to the public, it is situated on the Ring of Kerry and activities include horse riding on Rossbeigh beach (€25/hr), horse and pony trekking, crazy golf, pet corner and play area. Of special interest is a willow maze covering two acres of ground. Fun and games are organised in the maze with treasure hunts for groups.

Celtic and Prehistoric Museum

Kilvicadownig, Ventry, Dingle, Co. Kerry
Tel: 066-9159191
celticmuseum@hotmail.com   www.celticmuseum.com

- Open from March to 15 November, 10.00 to 5.30
- Adults, €4.00; Children, €2.50
- Located in Kilvicadownig, ten minutes west of Dingle

In the Celtic and Prehistoric Museum, visitors can enter the Fossil Room and walk on floors of 300 million-year-old sea worms. They can see a large nest of 70—80 million-year-old dinosaur eggs, a group of 500 million-year-old squid and the largest complete woolly mammoth skull in the world — the tusks are each ten feet long! Other highlights at the museum include fossil Ice Age beasts and authentic tools used by Homo Erectus, Neanderthal and Cro-Magnon man in the Cave Room. There is also 8,000 year old amber jewellery from Scandinavia, earth goddess figurines from Central Europe and stone battle axes and daggers introduced by invading horsemen from the east 4,500 years ago.

Coolwood Wildlife Park

Coolwood, Coolcaslagh, Killarney, Co Kerry
Tel: 064-36288   Fax: 064-50158

- Open during summer months (dates vary annually)
- Adults, €8.00; Children, €5.00; Family, €22.00
- Located two km off the N22 Killarney/Cork road near of Killarney

Coolwood is a 47-acre complex, seven acres of which is a wildlife park and the remaining 40 acres a wildlife sanctuary. Heavily wooded Coolwood is a stronghold of the red squirrel; ravens nest there in early spring as do jays, sparrowhawks, goldcrest, dippers and more common species. The wildlife park includes monkeys, wallabies, prairie dogs, agouti, arctic fox, maras, llama, capybara, mountjac deer, pygmy goats, miniature ponies, rhea, emu, fancy fowl, pigeons, a large bird-of-prey collection including golden eagle, large waterfowl collection, reptiles, pets' corner, and rabbittery. There is also a playground.

Crag Cave

Castleisland, Co Kerry
Tel: 066-7141244   Fax: 066-7142352
info@cragcave.com   www.cragcave.com

![HeritageISLAND IRELAND'S VISITOR ATTRACTIONS]

- Open March 17 to November 1, 10.00 to 6.00 (6.30 in July and August); rest of year enquire to number above
- Adults, €6.50; Children, €4.00; Family, €20.00
- Located two km outside Castleisland off N21
- Caters for children's parties
- Caters for school groups/tours

Crag Cave is a unique, all-weather visitor attraction at the gateway to County Kerry. Formed of limestone, it is a colourful wonderland of stalagmites and stalactites. Discovered in 1983 and thought to be over one million years old, this natural attraction has dramatic sound and lighting effects. A visit to Crag Cave will enthral all ages as guides explain the origins of the Cave, describe its many beautiful formations and introduce visitors to a world older than mankind. There is also an indoor soft play area for children under nine years (additional charge).

Derrynane House, National Historic Park

Caherdaniel, Co Kerry
Tel: 066-9475113   Fax: 066-9475432
www.heritageireland.ie

- Open May to September, 9.00 to 6.00; November to March, weekends, 1.00 to 5.00; April and October, Tuesday to Sunday, 1.00 to 5.00
- Adults, €2.75; Children, €1.25; Family, €7.00
- Located 3.5 km from Caherdaniel off N70 Ring of Kerry

Derrynane House is the ancestral home of Daniel O'Connell, lawyer, politician and statesman. The exhibition incorporates an audio-visual presentation and a guided tour on request. Today some 120 hectares of the lands of Derrynane, together with Derrynane House, make up Derrynane National Historic Park. Plantations and garden walks were laid out in the eighteenth and nineteenth centuries, principally north and west of the house. The main area of the gardens, set inland and to the north of the house, can be reached through a tunnel under the road. Access for visitors with disabilities to ground floor. *An OPW site.*

Dingle Oceanworld Aquarium

The Seafront, Dingle, Co Kerry
Tel: 066-9152111   Fax: 066-9152155
info@dingle-oceanworld.ie   www.dingle-oceanworld.ie

- Open May to June, September, 10.00 to 6.00; July to August, 10.00 to 8.30; October to April, 10.00 to 4.45
- Adults, €10.50; Children, €6.25;   Family Day-card, €28.50
- Located in Dingle, opposite the Marina
- Caters for children's parties
- Caters for school groups/tours

The Dingle Oceanworld Aquarium is home to over 100 species of fish and marine life. Visitors can meet tropical sharks who swim alongside turtles, feel the fish life in the touch pool, meet some spectacular seahorses and hold a starfish. Situated in the spectacular Dingle Peninsula, the aquarium is a perfect all-weather outing for young and old.

Fenit Sea World

The Pier, Fenit, Tralee, Co Kerry
Tel: 066-7136544   Fax: 066-7136544

- Open daily Easter to October, 11.00 to 5.30
- Contact Fenit for admission prices
- Located on the pier in Fenit
- Caters for children's parties
- Caters for school groups/tours

Fenit Sea World offers a unique opportunity to observe hundreds of species of underwater wildlife from Tralee Bay and the Atlantic Ocean. Visitors can wander through an amazing submarine labyrinth, explore the haunted timbers of an actual shipwreck, and experience a re-creation of the half-lit ocean floor where the habitat is both accessible and astonishingly natural. From tiny, delicate prawn to ferocious conger eel, from humble cod to rapacious shark, Fenit Sea World is entertainment and education, science and mystery, beauty and savagery. An experience not to be missed.

The Freshwater Experience

Emlagh, Lispole, Co Kerry
Tel: 066-9151042   Fax: 066-9151804
info@freshwaterexp.com

- Open March to October, Monday to Saturday, 9.30 to 6.00; Sunday, 12.00 to 6.00
- Contact for price information
- Located in Lispole

🍽 👫

Visitors to The Freshwater Experience can leave behind the modern world and walk into the Celtic past with examples of ancient Celtic monuments, including Ogham Stone, Wedge Tomb and Crannog, a medieval lake dwelling. There is also a wildfowl reserve which contains more than 30 species of duck, geese, and swans. The wildlife park also contains otters, foxes, wild boars, mink and other animals. The park also has a working trout farm where visitors can experience the sport and thrills of catching their own dinner.

The Great Blasket Centre

(Ionad an Bhlascaoid Mhóir) Dunquin, Tralee, Co Kerry
Tel: 066-9156444   Fax: 066-9156446
www.heritageireland.ie

- Open April to October, 10.00 to 5.15 (6.15 in July/August)
- Adults, €3.70; Children/Students, €1.30; Family, €8.70
- Located 10 miles west of Dingle town on the Slea Head drive
- Caters for school groups/tours

🍽 ♿ 👫 🎁

The magnificent Great Blasket Centre on the mainland in Dun Chaoin, Co Kerry, on the tip of the Dingle Peninsula, is a fascinating interpretative centre/museum, honouring the unique community who once lived on the remote Great Blasket Island. This community produced an extraordinary amount of literature, referred to as "The Blasket Library", which includes classics such as *The Islandman*, *Twenty Years A-Growing*, and *Peig*. Education pack available for secondary school children. *An OPW site.*

Kennedy's All Weather Pet Farm and Playground

Glenflesk, Killarney, Co Kerry
Tel 064-54054
kennedysfarm@eircom.net   www.killarneypetfarm.com

- Open daily year round, from 10.00 to 7.00
- Entrance fee €7.00 per person (includes free pony ride for children)
- Located six miles from Killarney on the Cork Road
- Caters for children's parties and school groups/tours
- Special programmes for children

🍽 ♿ 🚻 🎁

Kennedy's Pet Farm has pets of all kinds — deer, pigs, piglets, calves, sheep and lambs, goats and kids, rabbits, guinea pigs, ducks, geese, puppies and "Prince" the peacock — for children to cuddle, feed and play with. There are also two ponies for children to ride (no charge) and unique indoor and outdoor playgrounds to make for an unforgettable experience no matter the weather!

Kerry County Museum

Ashe Memorial Hall, Tralee, Co Kerry
Tel: 066-7127777   Fax: 066-7127444
kcmuseum@indigo.ie   www.kerrymuseum.ie

Heritage**ISLAND**
IRELAND'S VISITOR ATTRACTIONS

- Open daily June to August, 9.30 to 5.30; September to December, Tuesday to Saturday, 9.30 to 5.00; January to March, Tuesday to Friday, 10.00 to 4.30; April to May, Tuesday to Saturday, 9.30 to 5.30
- Adults, €8.00; Children, €5.00
- Located in centre of Tralee
- Caters for school groups/tours

🍽 ♿ 🚻 🎁

Kerry the Kingdom comprises three unique attractions combining audio-visual technology with life-size reconstructions and priceless archaeological treasures to trace man's history in Kerry from 5,000 BC to the present day. Among the centre's highlights is a time car ride through the reconstructed streets and houses of medieval Tralee. As visitors travel through the streets they will experience the sights, sounds and smells of the town on market day and witness the daily life of the townspeople.

Killarney Model Railway

Beech Road, Killarney, Co Kerry
Tel: 064-34000   Fax: 064-34000
kmodelrailway@eircom.net

- Open daily mid-March to October and throughout December, 10.30 to 6.00
- Contact for admission rates
- Located by the Tourist Information Centre at the New Street Car Park

Killarney Model Railway is one of the world's largest model railways. Over 50 trains running on over a mile of track transport visitors through the landmarks of Europe, from the snowy mountain tops of the Alps through Germany, France and England to the bustling town of Killarney itself. There are thousands of tiny people depicting all walks of life and a very impressive night time scene. Also available is a four-lane Scalextric race track for those who'd like to test racing skills.

Killarney National Park Education Centre

Knockreer House, Killarney, Co Kerry
Tel: 064-35960   Fax: 064-35960
knpeducationcentre@eircom.ie   www.homepage.tinet.ie/~knp

- Fees dependent on group size and activity
- Open year round.
- Located in Knockreer Demesne, opposite St Mary's Cathedral
- Caters for school groups/tours
- Special programmes for children

The Education Centre runs courses and activities within the National Park which promote knowledge, understanding, enjoyment and appreciation of the natural environment. The Centre runs Primary School Nature Days (ideal for a school tour), Leaving Cert Ecology and Geography Fieldwork Days and Discovery Weekends, which are aimed at scouts, guides and other youth groups.

Laser Combat Adventures

Upper Main Street, Waterville, Co Kerry
Loo Bridge, Killarney, Co Kerry
Tel: 066-9474465   Fax: 066-9474620
quadsafari@eircom.net   www.actionadventurecentre.com

- Open daily, 9.00 to 5.00
- €55 per person for three hours; €40 for two hours
- Located on Upper Main Street in Waterville
- Caters for children's parties
- Caters for school groups/tours
- Special programmes for children

The action adventure centre runs a state-of-the-art laser-combat game, "War Adventures". It is suitable for anyone from the age of ten upwards, and an active adventure for all the family to enjoy.

Listowel Heritage Town

Seanchaí — Kerry Literary and Cultural Centre, 24 The Square, Listowel, Co Kerry
Tel: 068-22212   Fax: 068-22170
info@kerrywritersmuseum.com
www.kerrywritersmuseum.com

HeritageISLAND
IRELAND'S VISITOR ATTRACTIONS

- Open daily June to September, 10.00 to 5.00; October to May, Monday to Friday, 10.00 to 4.00
- Adults, €5.00; Children, €3.00; Family, €12.00
- Located in Listowel town centre

Located on the banks of the River Feale, Listowel's long history dates back to 1303 where it first appears in the Plea Roll. Fortress to the Fitzmaurice family, the town developed around Listowel Castle and its magnificent square. Described as "the Literary Capital of Ireland", Listowel and North Kerry have produced some of Ireland's most distinguished writers including John B. Keane, Bryan MacMahon and Brendan Kennelly. These great literary figures are celebrated in a unique audio-visual experience at the Seanchaí — Kerry Literary and Cultural Centre. Other attractions include the unique Lartigue Monorailway and Listowel Castle.

Muckross Friary

Muckross Estate, Killarney, Co Kerry
Tel: 064-31440
www.heritageireland.ie

- Open daily mid-June to early September, 10.00 to 5.00
- No entrance fee
- Located four km from Killarney along the N71

This Franciscan Friary was founded in the fifteenth century and is in a remarkable state of preservation. The tower was added after the church was built and is the only Franciscan tower in Ireland which is as wide as the church. The cloister and its associated buildings are complete and an old yew tree stands in the centre. The monks were finally driven out by the Cromwellians in 1652. *An OPW site.*

Muckross House, Gardens and Traditional Farms and Craft Centre

Killarney National Park, Co Kerry
Tel: 064-31440   Fax: 064-37565
mucros@iol.ie   www.muckross-house.ie

- House and Gardens open year round, Farms open March to October
- Adults, €8.65; Children, €3.90; Family, €22.00 (admissions to House or Farms only available)
- Located within Killarney National Park

🍽️ 👫 🎁

Visitors to Muckross House will enjoy the elegantly furnished rooms which portray the lifestyles of the gentry and downstairs experience the working conditions of the servants employed in the house. At the Muckross Traditional Farms visitors can see three working farms from Kerry of the 1930s. Children will enjoy the various farm animals and the free trip on the Muckross Vintage Coach. There is also a Craft Centre with potters, weavers and bookbinders at work.

National Museum of Irish Transport

East Avenue Road, Killarney, Co Kerry
Tel: 064-34677
destinationkillarney@eircom.net

- Open daily May to September, 10.00 to 6.00; April and October, 11.00 to 5.00
- Contact for admission rates
- Located in centre of Killarney

Situated in the heart of Killarney town, this museum houses a marvellous collection of veteran and vintage transport, including cars, motorbikes, cycles, fire engines and even a 1930s workshop. All the vehicles are beautifully preserved. Included in the superb collection is the rarest car in the world, the 1907 Silver Stream (pictured above) of which only one was ever produced, and an 1898 Benz Velo, the first car to be driven in Ireland.

Ross Castle

Killarney, Co Kerry
Tel: 064-35851
www.heritageireland.ie

- Open daily April to May, 10.00 to 5.00; June to August, 9.00 to 6.30; October, Tuesday to Sunday, 10.00 to 5.00
- Adults, €5.30; Children, €2.10; Family, €11.50
- Located two km from Killarney on the N71

Ross Castle may be considered a typical example of the stronghold of an Irish chieftain during the Middle Ages. The date of its foundation is uncertain but it was probably built in the late fifteenth century by one of the O'Donoghue Ross chieftains. It is surrounded by a fortified bawn, its curtain walls defended by circular flanking towers, two of which remain. Much of the bawn was removed by the time the Barrack building was added on the south side of the castle sometime in the middle of the eighteenth century. Admission by guided tours only. Access for people with disabilities to the exhibition area on the ground floor. *An OPW site.*

Seafari Eco-Nature Cruises

The Pier, Kenmare, Co Kerry
Tel: 064-42059
seafari@eircom.net   www.seafariireland.com

- Open May to October, two to four cruises daily
- Adults, €20.00; Children, €12.50; Family, €60.00

Seafari, a two-hour eco-nature, history and seal-watching cruise, explores the many islands in Kenmare Bay's sheltered waters between the Beara and Iveragh mountain peninsulas. Visitors will see tropical plants nurtured by the Gulf Stream, prolific birdlife living off the productive seawater and observe from close-up Ireland's largest seal colony where 300 or more seals make their home. For children there are complimentary sweets, orange juice, a puppet show, face painting and free use of binoculars.

Siamsa Tíre

Town Park, Tralee, Co Kerry
Tel: 066-712 3055   Fax: 066-712 7276
siamsatire@eircom.net   www.siamsatire.com

Heritage**ISLAND**
IRELAND'S VISITOR ATTRACTIONS

- Open April to October; box office: Monday to Saturday, 9.00 to 6.00
- Contact Siamsa Tíre for costs
- Located in the Town Park in Tralee
- Caters for school groups/tours
- Special programmes for children

Siamsa Tíre is an arts centre facility which offers a forum for drama, music, dance, literary and the visual arts. It is also the home of the National Folk Theatre who present Irish folk culture in its many faceted forms, through the media of theatre and the traditional arts. Using the disciplines of traditional Irish music, dance, storytelling and mime, Siamsa Tíre offers a cultural experience dramatising the essence of the Irish people. A "Siamsa" show presents on stage the myths, legends, lore, language, folkways and folk life of a bygone era.

The Skellig Experience Centre

Valentia Island, Co Kerry
Tel: 066-9476306   Fax: 066-9476351
info@skelligexperience.com   www.skelligexperience.com

HeritageISLAND
IRELAND'S VISITOR ATTRACTIONS

- Open daily March to November, 10.00 to 5.00 (later summer openings from May)
- Adults, €5.00; Children, €3,00; Family, €14.00
- Located on the waterfront of Valentia Island, 11 km from the Ring of Kerry (N 70)
- Caters for school groups/tours
- Special programmes for children

At the Skellig Experience Centre visitors can learn about the offshore Skellig islands while remaining on dry land, in a custom-built, stone-clad, grass-roofed building on the waterfront beside the Valentia Island bridge. Through re-creations and models visitors can study the works and lives of the Skellig monks of the early Christian period, their activities, endurance and dedication in gaining a foothold on a tiny, inhospitable offshore island and creating a community there that survived for some 600 years. A 16-minute audio-visual presentation allows visitors to follow the footsteps of those Skellig monks, and wonder at the legacy of architecture that they left behind.

Adare Heritage Centre

Main Street, Adare, Co Limerick
Tel: 061-396666   Fax: 061-396932
adareheritage@eircom.net   www.heritageisland.com

HeritageISLAND
IRELAND'S VISITOR ATTRACTIONS

- Open daily year round, 9.00 to 6.00
- Adults, €5.00; Children, €3.50
- Located in centre of Adare village
- Caters for school groups/tours

Situated in Ireland's most picturesque village, the Adare Heritage Centre allows visitors to experience this area's unique history, spanning the years from 1233 to the present day. The story is told through realistic model enactments and audio-visuals in French, Italian, German, Irish and English. The centre also houses a Tourist Information Office, The Dovecot Restaurant, Black Abbey Crafts, Kerry Woollen Mills and Curran's Heraldry.

Foynes Flying Boat Museum

Foynes, Co Limerick
Tel: 069-65416
Email: famm@eircom.net
Web: www.flyingboatmuseum.com

Heritage**ISLAND**
IRELAND'S VISITOR ATTRACTIONS

- Open daily March 31 to October 31, 10.00 to 6.00
- Adults, €7.50; Children, €4.00; Family, €18.00
- Located 35 km west of Limerick on the N69.

Foynes became the centre of the aviation world when Pan Am's luxury Flying Boat, the *Yankee Clipper* landed there on 9 July 1939. This was the first commercial passenger flight on a direct route from the USA to Europe. During the late 1930s and early 1940s, this quiet little town on the Shannon became the focal point for air traffic on the North Atlantic. The Foynes Flying Boat Museum has a comprehensive range of exhibits and graphic illustrations. Visitors can travel back in time at the authentic 1940s cinema, to watch the award-winning film "Atlantic Conquest". The museum showcases the original Terminal Building, Radio and Weather Room, complete with transmitters, receivers and Morse code equipment.

Hunt Museum

The Custom House, Rutland Street, Limerick
Tel: 061-312833   Fax: 061-312834
reservations@huntmuseum.com   www.huntmuseum.com

Heritage**ISLAND**
IRELAND'S VISITOR ATTRACTIONS

- Open Monday to Saturday, 10.00 to 5.00; Sunday, 2.00 to 5.00
- Adults, €7.20; Children, €3.50
- Caters for children's parties
- Caters for school groups/tours
- Special programmes for children

The Hunt Museum is a treasure house of artefacts from all over the world acquired by John and Gertrude Hunt. All young visitors to the museum are invited to participate in the Hunt Museum Treasure Trail. Colouring sheets are available for the very young. Booked groups have the option of participating in a variety of workshops such as a costume or portrait workshop, a Medieval or Prehistoric workshop or the recently developed Time Travel workshop.

Irish Palatine Museum

Old Railway Buildings, Rathkeale, Co Limerick
Tel: 069-63511
ipass@eircom.net   www.irishpalatines.org

- Open May to September, Tuesday to Saturday and Bank Holiday
  Mondays, 2.00 to 5.00; other times by arrangement
- Adults, €5.00; Students, €3.00; Family, €12.00
- Located on the N21 at Rathkeale, 29 km from Limerick City
- Caters for school groups/tours

In 1709 several hundred families of German origin settled in Ireland. Known as the Palatines, they established roots mainly in Counties Limerick, Kerry, Tipperary and Wexford. The centre houses an exhibition which seeks to represent in detail the Irish Palatine experience ranging from their German places of origin to their colonisation and settlement in Ireland, and their subsequent scattering all over the English-speaking world. The Centre features an extensive display of artefacts, photographs, graphics etc. associated with the Palatine story.

Limerick City Gallery of Art

Carnegie Building, Pery Square, Limerick City
Tel: 061-310633
artgallery@limerickcity.ie   www.limerickcity.ie/LCGA

- Open Monday to Friday, 10.00 to 6.00; Thursday,
  10.00 to 7.00; Saturday, 10.00 to 5.00; Sunday,
  2.00 to 5.00
- Admission is free
- Located in the People's Park, near Railway Station
- Caters for school groups/tours

Limerick City Gallery of Art has a fine permanent collection of works by early eighteenth-, nineteenth- and twentieth-century Irish artists, which encourages the visitor to trace the development of modern Irish art in painting, sculpture and drawing. The collection, begun in 1948, continues to grow each year. The Gallery also hosts exciting contemporary exhibitions by Irish and international artists including the widely known ev+a exhibition.

King John's Castle

King's Island, Nicholas Street, Limerick City
Tel: 061-411201   Fax: 061-361020
www.shannonheritage.com

ℍeritageISLAND
IRELAND'S VISITOR ATTRACTIONS

- Open daily May to August, 10.00 to 5.30; April, September, October, 10.00 to 5.00; November to March, 10.30 to 4.30
- Adults, €8.35; Children, €4.95; Family, €20.45
- Located in Limerick City
- Caters for school groups/tours

♿ 🚻 🎁

The Castle was built between 1200 and 1210 and was repaired and extended many times in the following centuries. The interpretive centre at the Castle contains an imaginative historical exhibition which tells the story of the Castle. Archaeological excavations have revealed pre-Norman settlements and evidence from the traumatic siege of 1642. The courtyard and the Castle display some of the trades and traditions of the sixteenth century. The Castle offers panoramic views of Limerick city and the surrounding countryside.

Limerick Museum

Castle Lane, Nicholas Street, Limerick City
Tel: 061-417826   Fax: 061-415266
lwalsh@limerickcorp.ie   www.limerickcity.ie

- Open year round, Tuesday to Saturday, 10.00 to 1.00 and 2.15 to 5.00
- No entrance fee
- Located beside King John's Castle in Limerick
- Caters for school groups/tours

♿ 🚻

Limerick Museum's collection of almost 30,000 objects illustrates the past of the city and region, from earliest times to the present day. The main themes in the collection are Archaeology of the Mid-West region, History of Limerick Corporation, including city charters from Charles II and Oliver Cromwell, the civic sword granted by Elizabeth I, the city maces made by the Limerick silversmith, John Robinson, and the famous Nail from the City Exchange. Many fine examples of Limerick Lace, a craft which began in the city in 1829, are also on display.

Peter Pan Fun World

Dooradoyle, Co Limerick
Tel: 061-301033   Fax: 091-790608

- Open daily 10.00 to 7.00
- €7.00 per hour (Group rates available)
- Located in the Crescent Shopping Centre, Dooradoyle
- Caters for children's parties
- Caters for school groups/tours

This action-packed indoor play centre offers a soft play area for the under-fives and "Adventureland", a multi-faceted play area for five- to ten-year-olds. Features include a 60-foot snake slide, a freefall slide, a triple-lane Astra slide, tunnel slides, two large ball-pools, a haunted cave, rope-bridges and scramble nets. Birthday catering with special play rates provides everything except the cake.

Stonehall Visitor Farm

Kilcornan, Co Limerick
Tel: 061-393940
stonehallvisitorfarm@eircom.net   www.stonehallvisitorfarm.com

- Open daily July, August, 11.00 to 6.00; open weekends April–June, September, 12.00 to 6.00
- €6.00 per person
- Located on N69, Curraghchase, Kilcornan
- Caters for children's parties
- Caters for school groups/tours
- Provides guided tours

The farm has a wide variety of animals and birds, including llama, alpacas, deer, chinchillas, parrots, ostrich, emu, rhea and eagle owl. There are also many nature trails and walks for fine weather. Indoors, a play area provides a range of toys and amusements including a bouncy castle and "rough riders". Picnic areas available indoors and out. Baby changing and coach and car parking facilities.

Tons of Fun Children's Activity Centre

Unit H1 Eastway Business Park, Tipperary Road, Limerick
Tel: 061-431141
info@tonsoffun.ie   www.tonsoffun.ie

- Open Monday to Saturday 10.00 to 6.00, Sundays and Bank Holidays 11.00 to 6.00
- For one hour's play: Children, €7; Group rates available
- Located three km from Limerick City Centre, off the Tipperary Road (N24),
- Caters for school groups tours
- Caters for school groups

A safe, clean and supervised indoor softplay and adventure experience for children aged 0-11 years. Play areas include: three-level climbing maze, ball jugglers, ball lifters and ball pools, tubular and wavy slides, cannons firing foam balls, roller racer track. Private party rooms, comfortable seating area for adults, coffee shop serving drinks and light snacks.

Brú Ború Cultural Centre

Cashel, Co Tipperary
Tel: 062-61122   Fax: 062-62700
bruboru@comhaltas.com   www.comhaltas.com

HeritageISLAND
IRELAND'S VISITOR ATTRACTIONS

- Open daily mid-June to mid-September, 9.00 to 11.30 pm (shows Tuesday to Saturday); rest of year, Monday to Friday, 9.00 to 5.00 (no shows)
- Admission to Centre only is free; "Sounds of History": Adults, €5.00; Children, €3.00
- Located beneath the Rock of Cashel
- Caters for school groups tours

The Sounds of History exhibition, located in the subterranean chambers seven metres underground at the base of the Rock of Cashel, echo to the story of Ireland from ancient times to the present day. Visitors will be introduced to some of the main characters of Ireland's story — St Patrick, King Aengus, Myler McGrath, Lord Inchiquin, Brian Ború, Queen Gormlaith and others — as well as some of the great music personalities from Bunting at the Belfast Harp Festival to Captain Francis O'Neill in Chicago.

Cahir Castle

Castle Street, Cahir, Co Tipperary
Tel: 052-41011   Fax: 052-42324
www.heritageireland.ie

- Open daily mid-June to mid-September, 9.00 to 7.00; rest of year, 9.30 to 5.30 (4.30 in winter)
- Adults, €2.90; Children, €1.30; Family, €7.40
- Located in the centre of Cahir town
- Caters for school groups/tours
- Special programmes for children

Once the stronghold of the powerful Butler family, Cahir Castle is one of Ireland's largest and best-preserved castles. Visitors can explore the castle with wall walks, spooky stairs, creaky doors, prison towers and murder holes and hear tour guides talk about life in the Middle Ages. They can also see how the castle was attacked in miniature with 1,000 toy soldiers and search for a real cannon ball. The castle's attractions include an excellent audio-visual show which informs visitors of all the main sites of the area. *An OPW site.*

Cashel Heritage Centre

Cashel, Co Tipperary
Tel: 062-61333   Fax: 062-61333
cashelhc@iol.ie   www.cashel.ie

HeritageISLAND
IRELAND'S VISITOR ATTRACTIONS

- Open 9.30 to 5.30, mid-March to mid-October, daily; mid-October to mid-March, Monday to Friday
- No entrance fee
- Located at City Hall, Main Street, Cashel
- Caters for school groups/tours

An audio-visual tour gives the history of Cashel in the 1640s in seven languages. Charters of Cashel are on permanent display and a large-scale model of the town in former years highlights some lesser-known treasures.

Lár na Páirce — The Story of Gaelic Games

Thurles, Co Tipperary
Tel: 0504-22702   Fax: 0504-24333
tippgaa@eircom.net   www.tipperary.gaa.ie

- Open Monday to Friday year round, Saturdays from April to September, 10.00 to 5.00
- Contact the centre for admission costs
- Located in Thurles near Liberty Square
- Caters for school groups/tours

Lár na Páirce is a Visitor Centre designed and equipped to tell the story of Gaelic games from earliest times. The exhibits housed in the centre display hurling, Gaelic football, camogie and handball and extend to Cúchulainn, landlords, hurley-making and broadcasting. Of particular interest is the famous Sam Melbourne Collection, a personal lifetime collection of sporting memorabilia.

Mitchelstown Cave

Burncourt, Cahir, Co Tipperary
Tel: 052-67246   Fax: 052-67943

- Open all year, 10.00 to 6.00
- Contact about admission rates
- Located midway between Cahir and Mitchelstown
- Caters for school groups/tours
- Provides guided tours

Visitors, groups and school outings are shown daily through approx. half a mile of this world-famous cave. Visitors stroll in comfort through three massive caverns viewing dripstone formations, stalactites, stalagmites, graceful calcite curtains hanging from sloping roofs, calcite crystals that glisten like diamonds and the nine-metre high "Tower of Babel", one of Europe's finest calcite columns. The temperature inside the cave remains constant at 12 degrees centigrade, making it an ideal all-weather tourist attraction.

Ormond Castle

Castle Park, Carrick-on-Suir, Co Tipperary
Tel: 051-640787
www.heritageireland.ie

- Open daily mid-June to early September, 9.30 to 6.30
- Adults, €2.90; Children, €1.30; Family, €7.40
- Located off Castle Street in Carrick-on-Suir

♿ ♀♂

Ormond Castle is the best example of an Elizabethan manor house in Ireland. It was built by Thomas, the tenth Earl of Ormond in the 1560s. Closely integrated into the manor house are two fifteenth century towers. It is the country's only major unfortified dwelling from that turbulent period. The state rooms contain some of the finest decorative plasterwork in the country, including plasterwork portraits. Restricted access for visitors with disabilities. *An OPW site.*

Parson's Green Leisure Park

Clogheen, Co Tipperary
Tel: 052-65290   Fax: 052-65504
kathleennoonan@oceanfree.net   www.clogheen.com

- Open March 17 to September 30, 10.00 to 8.00
- Adults, €3.00, Children, €2.50, Family, €12.00
- Located in Clogheen, SW of Cahir
- Caters for children's parties
- Caters for school groups/tours

🍽 ♿ ♀♂ 🎁

Parson's Green is a family-run park at the foot of Knockmealdown Mountains and bounded by the River Tar. Included in the park are garden and river walks, a pet farm, a farm museum, crazy golf, playgrounds, trap, boat and pony rides, a wendy house, toddlers' sandpit, and a Viking sweat house. There is also a caravan and camping park and mobile homes and apartments.

Rock of Cashel

Cashel, Co Tipperary
Tel: 062-61437   Fax: 062-62988
www.heritageireland.ie

- Open daily mid-June to mid-September, 9.00 to 7.00; mid-September to mid-March, 9.00 to 4.30; mid-March to mid-June, 9.00 to 5.30
- Adults, €5.30; Children, €2.10; Family, €11.50
- Located 500 metres from centre of Cashel off the Dublin road

One of Ireland's most popular attractions, the Rock of Cashel includes a spectacular group of medieval buildings set on an outcrop of limestone in the Golden Vale including the twelfth-century round tower, High Cross and Romanesque Chapel, thirteenth-century Gothic cathedral, fifteenth-century Castle and the restored Hall of the Vicars Choral. Attractions include an audio-visual show, "Stonghold of the Faith", and exhibitions. Access for visitors with disabilities by prior arrangement. *An OPW site.*

Roscrea Castle and Damer House

Castle Street, Roscrea, Co Tipperary
Tel: 0505-21850   Fax: 0505-21904

- Open mid-March to end of October, 10.00 to 6.00
- Adults, €3.70; Children, €1.30; Family, €8.70
- Located in centre of Roscrea town
- Caters for school groups/tours
- Special programmes for children (on request)

Roscrea Castle dates back to the thirteenth century and has many interesting passages and dungeons to explore. The castle consists of a large walled enclosure with a massive rectangular gatehouse on one side. The gatehouse has a drawbridge and portcullis (lifting gate) which were reconstructed in the early 1990s. Damer House is an eighteenth century town house in the castle grounds with formal gardens, fountains and many interesting exhibitions.

Tuning Children into Nature

Paddy Madden

As a child I was lucky: I had three people in my life who helped me to see the world around me. My father and mother unveiled the mysteries of nature to me in incidental ways: they pointed out an insect here, a tree there . . . it was easy learning, never hurried.

My teacher in the senior classes in primary school, Pake Haran, had a huge influence too in unlocking my natural intelligence. Most days we brought in leaves, flowers etc. and left them on his desk "to keep him talking". He would take up the samples first thing in the morning and with the help of some charts he would guide us through their identification and habitats. He pretended to be just as ignorant as us about them which I now know was a teaching strategy. By "keeping him talking" we devious pupils kept him away from the dreaded "sums" and "Irish" as long as possible!

Those fragile beginnings made me and many more from that small rural school into life-long naturalists. Experience since has taught me that those three people knew the secret of successful environmental education: open all the child's senses early to the world about him. One doesn't have to be able to identify anything; all that matters is interest and enthusiasm. Kavanagh in his poem "On Reading A Book On Common Wild Flowers" sums this point up beautifully:

> "I knew them all by eyesight long before I knew their names,
> We were in love before we were introduced."

Of course it is important to get out and about with the children. The books and videos should come *after* the outdoor ventures. A look around the back garden, a walk in a park, a visit to a wood, an exploration of a water feature . . . these are the blackboards of nature learning.

The living things under soil, stones and bark, in rotting logs and ponds and old stone walls, on branch and leaf offer infinite possibilities. Let the children observe and explore; let them hear and smell; let them question and research.

Konrad Lorenz wrote: "Whoever has seen the intimate beauty of nature cannot tear themselves away from it again and again. They must become either a poet or a naturalist, and if their eyes are good and their powers of observation sharp enough, they may well become both."

A child who grows things too will observe nature closely. Give him a little piece of garden to grow annuals and vegetables. Make a wigwam or a bamboo tunnel and sow peas or beans. If no ground is available let him sow seeds in empty yoghurt containers or used mushroom trays. Sunflowers are a must. Sow these indoors in April and plant them outside in May.

Respect for trees comes from watching them grow. So . . . let him grow an oak from seed. Find an empty one-litre milk carton in autumn. Pierce some holes in the bottom for drainage. Place some pebbles over the holes. Fill with potting compost leaving some space at the top for watering. Insert an acorn that hasn't been allowed to dry out. Water and cover with perforated cling film to prevent moisture loss. Leave it indoors over the winter and it will germinate in the spring. Tell him that the tree has begun a journey that may last for 800 years. Living trees are safe in the hands of children who grow trees from seed. Vandals of the future will not come from the ranks of tree growers.

What material presents might one buy to encourage a child along nature's way? A good set of binoculars if you can afford them; a good magnifying glass and a notebook and pencil if you can't. These tools assist *observation* and observation is the key that unlocks the wonderful world of nature.

A respect and love of nature is a great gift to give to a child. The world is an open book to him and his days are filled. Certainly, the bleak, empty, spiritless words "I am bored" will seldom emit from the lips of a child of nature.

Paddy Madden lectures on the Environment in Marino Institute of Education. He is the author of Go Wild at School *and* The School Garden: What to do and When to do it.

Roscrea Heritage Town

Castle Street, Roscrea, Co Tipperary
Tel: 0505-21850   Fax: 0505-21904
roscreaheritage@opw.ie   www.roscreaonline.com

HeritageISLAND
IRELAND'S VISITOR ATTRACTIONS

- Open daily mid-March to October 31, 10.00 to 6.00
- Adults, €3.50; Children, €1.25; Family, €8.25
- Located in Roscrea town centre

Roscrea has a proud and ancient history going back many centuries. A great way to explore Roscrea is the Heritage Walk, starting at the restored thirteenth-century Castle in the town centre. All visitors should take time to see Monaincha Abbey with its Hiberno-Romanesque carvings and savour the pilgrim spirit which has prevailed here for centuries. Roscrea's monastic tradition was re-established over 100 years ago by the Cistercians with their abbey and school. Mount St Joseph's is set in beautiful grounds four km from the town and is a haven of peace and tranquility.

South Tipperary County Museum

Mick Delahunty Square, Clonmel, Co Tipperary
Tel: 052-34550
museum@southtippcoco.ie   www.southtippcoco.ie

- Open year round Tuesday to Saturday
- No entrance fee
- Located beside the swimming pool in Clon-mel town
- Caters for school groups/tours
- Special programmes for children

The South Tipperary County Museum, the first custom-built county museum in the country, has two exhibition galleries, one of which has a permanent display of objects from Tipperary's history and the other which is used for temporary exhibitions. The museum has an outreach programme with workshops and talks which are aimed at all ages. A worksheet is available for both primary and secondary students and facilities for colouring are available for younger children.

Swiss Cottage

Kilcommon, Cahir, Co Tipperary
Tel: 052-41144
www.heritageireland.ie

- Open daily May to mid-October, 10.00 to 6.00; open Tuesday to Sunday, 10.00 to 1.00 and 2.00 to 4.30, mid-October to November, mid-March to April
- Adults, €2.90; Children, €1.30; Family, €7.40
- Located 1.5 km south of Cahir off R670

A delightful "cottage orné" built in the early 1800s by Richard Butler, first Earl of Glengall, to a design by the famous Regency architect John Nash. Its interior contains a graceful spiral staircase and some elegantly decorated rooms. The wallpaper in the Salon manufactured by the Dufour factory is one of the first commercially produced Parisian wallpapers. Situated on an elevated site with access by stone steps. *An OPW site.*

Tipperary Excel Heritage Centre

Mitchell Street, Tipperary
Tel: 062-80520   Fax: 062-80550
info@tipperary-excel.com   www.tipperary-excel.com

HeritageISLAND
IRELAND'S VISITOR ATTRACTIONS

- Open Monday to Saturday 9.30 to 5.30
- Admission is free
- Located beside the Market Square in the centre of Tipperary Town

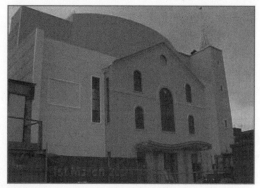

The Interpretative Centre in the Excel Centre features an interactive multimedia presentation telling the story of Tipperary past and present. Visitors can spend an hour experiencing the unique features that represent Tipperary Town, its surroundings and its people. The Tipperary Excel Centre also includes an art gallery, cinema, theatre and family history research centre.

Copper Coast European Geopark

Information Centre, Knockmahon Lodge, Bunmahon, Co Waterford.
Tel: 051-292828   Fax: 051-292820
info@coppercoastgeopark.com   www.coppercoastgeopark.com

- Open year round
- No admission fee
- The Geopark area runs from west of Tramore (R675) to Stradbally
- Caters for school groups/tours
- Special programmes for children

The Copper Coast European Geopark is an outdoor museum comprising 25 kilometres of spectacular coastline, where you can visit sites of ancient volcanoes, touch stones created 460 million years ago and discover fossils. There are weekly guided walks and family and child-centred events as part of the summer programme. During the last week in May, European Geopark Week is celebrated with workshops, exhibitions, guided walks and talks. The Copper Coast was awarded European Geopark Status in 2001 and UNESCO Global Geopark Status in 2004.

Copper Coast Mini Farm

Fenore, Tramore, Co Waterford
Tel: 051-396870   Fax: 051-396869
coppercoastminifarm@eircom.net

- Open Easter, May 1 to September 1, Monday to Saturday, 10.00 to 6.00; Sunday and Bank Holidays, 12.00 to 6.00
- Adults, €5.50; Toddlers, €4.50
- Located five km from Tramore on R675
- Caters for school groups/tours

Copper Coast Mini Farm has friendly animals to pet and feed: donkeys, ponies, chinchillas, ducks, geese, jersey cows, and squirrels. There are toy tractors and diggers to drive, indoor and outdoor sandpits, a playhouse, toys and colouring fun. There is a special Easter egg hunt annually with games, prizes, face painting and races. Santa visits in December with quality presents and there is a live stable of Bethlehem.

Lismore Heritage Town

Lismore Heritage Centre, Lismore, Co Waterford
Tel: 058-54975   Fax: 058-53009
lismoreheritage@eircom.net   www.lismoreheritage.com

- Open all year, Monday to Friday, 9.30 to 5.30;
  May to October, Saturday, 10.00 to 5.30,
  Sunday 12.00 to 5.30
- Adults, €4.50; Children, €4.00; Family,
  €12.00
- Located in the old courthouse in Lismore
- Caters for school groups/tours
- Special programmes for children

An award-winning multimedia presentation takes the visitor on an enthralling journey through time, starting with the arrival of St Carthage in 636. The "Lismore Experience" is an ideal point of departure from which to explore the ancient treasures of the town and its surrounding countryside. Hear the strange story of the "Book of Lismore", dating back 1,000 years, and of the Lismore Crozier from 1116, both of which were discovered hidden in the walls of Lismore Castle in 1814. Guided school tours including a nature trail, tour of the town and cathedral, and puppet making are available.

Splashworld

Tramore, Co Waterford
Tel: 051-390176   Fax: 051-390214
info@splashworld.ie   www.splashworld.ie

- Open daily, year-round
- Contact for admission rates
- Located at Railway Square, Tramore, ten km
  from Waterford City
- Caters for children's parties
- Caters for school groups/tours
- Has special programmes for children

The southeast's biggest waterpark has a wealth of water-rides, including an indoor/outdoor helter skelter ride, splash slides, a wave pool, bubble pool, roaring rapids, water cannon, and a "pirate ship", along with gentler water fun and a splash pool for babies.

Waterford County Museum

Old Town Hall, St Augustine Street, Dungarvan, Co Waterford
Tel: 058-45960
history@waterfordcountymuseum.com   www.waterfordcountymuseum.com

- Open Monday to Friday, 10.00 to 5.00; June to September open Saturdays, 1.00 to 5.00
- Admission is free
- Located opposite the Augustinian Church in Dungarvan
- Caters for school groups/tours

The aim of the Waterford County Museum is to preserve the history of County Waterford; acquire, record and preserve individual items and collections of local interest; encourage public interest in local history; and publish various books and pamphlets on subjects of historical and local interest. The museum has two websites, waterfordcountymuseum.org, which contains over 3,500 pages of Waterford history, and waterfordcountyimages.org, which contains over 2,000 images of Co Waterford and was recently awarded Best Small Museum Website 2006 at the Museums and the Web International Conference.

Waterford Crystal Visitor Centre

Kilbarry, Waterford
Tel: 051-332500   Fax: 051-332716
visitorreception@waterford.ie
www.waterfordvisitorcentre.com

HeritageISLAND
IRELAND'S VISITOR ATTRACTIONS

- Showrooms open daily March to October, 8.30 to 6.00; November to February, 9.00 to 5.00
- Adults, €7.00; Children under 12, free
- Located 2 miles outside Waterford city
- Caters for school groups/tours

The Waterford Crystal Visitor Centre includes a splendid new showroom where the many prestigious pieces presented to presidents, sport stars and celebrities are showcased. The Waterford Crystal experience is unique in that visitors are visiting a real working, living, breathing factory. There is also the opportunity to experience the magic and excitement of the Times Square celebrations in New York, in a specially constructed room, with a replica of the ball which descended to officially welcome the new millennium in New York.

Waterford and Suir Railway

Kilmeadan, Co Waterford
Tel: 051-384058   Fax: 051-876002
wsvr@waterfordchamber.ie   www.wsvrailway.ie

- Open April to September, Monday to Saturday, 11.00 to 4.00 and Sundays 12.00 to 5.00; "Santa trips" run in December
- Adults, €7.00; Children, €3.50; Family, €16.00
- Located at Kilmeadan station, one mile up the R680 from the Cork/Waterford road (N25).
- Caters for children's parties
- Caters for school groups/tours

A t Kilmeadan station begins a 40-minute trip on this old-fashioned diesel railway, travelling at ten miles per hour through the countryside, passing farms, an equestrian centre, and alongside the River Suir for glimpses of cormorants, herons and reed buntings, and finally the Woodstown Viking site. A refurbished railway carriage at the station is available for children's parties.

Waterford Museum of Treasures and Reginald's Tower

Merchant's Quay, Waterford
Tel: 051-304500   Fax: 051-304501
mail@waterfordtreasures.com   www.waterfordtreasures.com

- Open daily June to August, 9.30 to 9.00; May, September, 9.30 to 6.00; October to April, 10.00 to 5.00
- Museum: Adults, €7.00; Children, €3.20 (under-five free); Family, €15.00–€21.00. Tower: Adults, €2.10; Children, €1.10; Family, €5.80
- Caters for school groups/tours

T he Waterford Museum of Treasures includes Viking jewellery, the magnificently illustrated fourteenth century Great Charter Roll and Henry VIII's cap of maintenance. The Museum celebrates the story of Ireland's oldest city, aided by seven audio-visual displays and interactive pods. Visitors can also see Reginald's Tower, first built by the Vikings, which has stood on this site like a Colossus protecting the quays of Waterford. The present structure has recently been completely restored to its medieval appearance and houses an elegant new exhibition which tells the story of the tower which functioned as a fortress, a mint, a prison and a museum.

For the Kids in Ulster

Ardclinis Outdoor Adventure

11 High Street, Cushendall, Co Antrim
Tel: 028-21771340   Fax: 028-21771340
ardclinis@aol.com   www.ardclinis.com

- Open year round 9.00 to 7.00
- Fees vary depending on activity
- Several locations around Co Antrim (see website)
- Suitable for children 8+
- Caters for children's parties
- Caters for school groups/tours
- Special programmes for children

Ardclinis provides a wide variety of outdoor activities, all with qualified instructors. Activities include archery, rope course, canoeing, climbing and abseiling, bridge building and orienteering. Older children can take part in powerboat handling courses.

Belfast Exposed Photography

The Exchange Place, 23 Donegall Street, Belfast
Tel: 028-90230965
info@belfastexposed.org   www.belfastexposed.org

- Open Tuesday to Saturday, 11.00 to 5.00
- Admission is free

♿ 🚻

Belfast Exposed is a photographic resource, archive and gallery; it remains Northern Ireland's only dedicated photography gallery. The Exchange Place now houses a 7x20 metre gallery for the exhibition of contemporary photography, a spacious black-and-white photographic darkroom and an eight-person Apple Mac digital suite. Through its annual programme of exhibitions and the commissioning of new work, Belfast Exposed promotes excellence, access and participation in the arts and aims to raise the profile of photography as an art form.

Belfast Zoo

Antrim Road, Newtownabbey, Co Antrim
Tel: 028-90776277   Fax: 028-90370578
strongej@belfastcity.gov.uk   www.belfastzoo.co.uk

- Open daily April to September, 10.00 to 7.00 (last admission 5.00); October to March, 10.00 to 4.00
- Contact Zoo for current prices
- Caters for children's parties
- Caters for school groups/tours

🍽 ♿ 🚻 🎁

Belfast Zoo is a world-class zoo which offers an entertaining and educational experience to visitors. It houses animals from all over the world, including "Big Cats", primates of all shapes and sizes, an African enclosure with giraffes, elephants and zebra, penguins, sea lions and an array of birds from every continent. Belfast Zoo also houses many endangered species from across the world and visitors get a chance to enjoy and learn about these fascinating animals and contribute to their survival.

Carnfunnock Country Park

Coast Road, Larne, Co Antrim
Tel: 028-28270541   Fax: 028-28270852
larnetourism@btconnect.com   www.larne.gov.uk

- Open 9.00 to 5.00; April to September, Monday to Saturday;October to March, Monday to Friday. Bank holidays, 10.00 to 4.00
- Costs vary per activity; please enquire
- Located 3.5 miles from Larne on the Antrim Coast Road
- Caters for children's parties
- Caters for school groups/tours
- 🍽 🚻 🎁

Carnfunnock Country Park consists of 473 acres of mixed woodland, colourful gardens, ponds, walking trails, beaches and activities for the whole family. For children there is an Activity Centre with an outdoor adventure playground, crazy golf, giant chess set, table tennis and a putting green. There is also a maze — sculpted in the shape of Northern Ireland — a miniature railway, bouncy castle, walled garden and a nine-hole par-3 golf course. Events take place regularly throughout the year.

Carrick-a-Rede

Whitepark Road, Ballintoy, Co Antrim
Tel: 028-20731582   Fax: 028-20769839
carrickarede@nationaltrust.org.uk   www.nationaltrust.org.uk

- Open June to August 10.00 to 7.00; September to May, 10.00 to 6.00
- Rope bridge: Adults, £2.50; Children, £1.30; Family, £6.30. Group rates available
- Located just east of Ballintoy
- Caters for school groups/tours
- 🍽 ♿ 🚻

On the North Antrim Coastal Path, just east of Ballintoy, is one of Northern Ireland's best-loved attractions: the Carrick-a-Rede rope bridge. Salmon fishermen sling this precarious bridge to the island over a chasm that is 24 metres deep and 18 metres wide. Those bold enough to cross are rewarded with fantastic views and wildlife.

Carrickfergus Castle

Marine Highway, Carrickfergus, Co Antrim
Tel: 028-93351273
www.ehsni.gov.uk/places/monuments

- Open April to September, Monday to Saturday, 10.00 to 6.00; Sunday, 2.00 to 6.00 (12.00 to 6.00 in summer); October to March, Monday to Saturday, 10.00 to 4.00; Sunday, 2.00 to 4.00
- Adults, £3.00; Children, £1.50; Family, £8.00
- Located north of Belfast on the A2
- Caters for children's parties

A striking feature of the landscape from land, sea and air, Carrickfergus Castle greets all visitors with its strength and menace. As visitors walk around the Castle they will find model historic figures that bring its stormy history to life. From the Norman knight, John de Courcy, and his wife Lady Affreca to guards at their posts keeping watch over the Castle, these life-size models portray the characters that make up the Castle's history. Most activities are to be found in the Keep where visitors may come across an armour demonstration or try their hand at medieval writing or medieval games.

Carrickfergus Museum

11 Antrim Street, Carrickfergus, Co Antrim
Tel: 028-93358000
info@carrickfergus.org   www.carrickfergus.org

- Open Monday to Friday, 9.00 to 5.00; Saturday, 10.00 to 5.00
- No entrance fee
- Located in Carrickfergus city centre
- Caters for school groups/tours
- Special programmes for children

Carrickfergus Museum and Civic Centre was opened on 24 March 2005. The museum's purpose is to interpret the long and distinguished history of the town and surrounding area from the earliest times to the present day. The main display gallery shows artefacts belonging to the Council's own civic collection as well as important material on loan from both private and national collections. There are several "hands-on" interactive facilities giving a fun as well as an informative angle to the displays. The museum's education room provides the base for curriculum-linked education programmes, which includes workshops for schools and associated resource materials.

Colin Glen Trust

163 Stewartstown Road
Dunmurry, Belfast, Co Antrim
Tel: 028-90614115   Fax: 028-90601694
info@colinglentrust.org   www.colinglentrust.org

- Open year round
- No entrance fee
- Located in Blefast adjacent to M1 motorway
- Caters for children's parties
- Caters for school groups/tours
- Special programmes for children

The Colin Glen Forest Park offers minibeast studies, tree and wildflower identification, sensory walks, eco-trails and teddy bear picnics throughout the year. All programmes are guided by Educational Rangers at this European award-winning forest park. The Forest Park is accessible from the Belfast Hills to the River Lagan and visitors can even collect fossils along the route of the Colin River.

Dundonald International Ice Bowl

111 Old Dundonald Road, Belfast
Tel: 028-90809100   Fax: 028-90489604
sales@castlereagh.gov.uk   www.theicebowl.com

- Open daily year round
- Costs vary, please telephone
- Located five miles from city centre
- Caters for children's parties
- Caters for school groups/tours

🍽 ♿ 🚻

Dundonald International Ice Bowl includes an Olympic-size ice rink, ten-pin bowling, an indoor adventure playground and crèche facilities. Ice-skating lessons are available and kids can join the Polar Bear Club, an activity-based children's club held every Saturday. Birthday parties are a speciality with themed party rooms including the Polar Bear Room, Indies Castle, Indies Jungle and Pins Bumper Room.

Dunluce Castle

Dunluce, Co Antrim
Tel: 028-20731938
www.northantrim.com/dunlucecastle.htm

- Open April to September, Monday to Saturday, 10.00 to 6.00; Sunday, 2.00 to 6.00 (12.00 to 6.00 in summer); October to March, Tuesday to Saturday, 10.00 to 4.00; Sunday, 2.00 to 4.00
- Adults, £1.50; Children, £0.75
- Located two miles west of Bushmills

• ♿ 🚻 🎁

This late-medieval and seventeenth-century castle is dramatically sited on a headland dropping sheer into the sea on the north Antrim Coast. It creates an exciting image of danger and adventure backed up by its history. The buildings on the rock are almost all of sixteenth/early-seventeenth-century date. Slight earthworks, visible to the west of the castle, are remains of a formal garden and part of the long-deserted town, whose ruined church stands in the graveyard south of the castle.

The Dunluce Centre

10 Sandhill Drive, Portrush, Co Antrim
Tel: 028-70824444   Fax: 028-70822256
www.dunlucecentre.co.uk

- Open daily Easter to August; early April and September-October, weekends only; opening hours vary.
- Individual tickets, £3.50 to £4.50; inclusive tickets, £8.50; Family tickets, from £27.00
- Caters for children's parties
- Caters for school groups/tours

Winner of the Best Visitor Attraction in Northern Ireland for 2002, the Dunluce Centre's attractions include Turbo Tours, a motion simulation ride; Finn McCool's Adventure Playground, the biggest indoor play structure in Ireland at three storeys high; Treasure Fortress, a unique medieval themed electronic treasure hunt; and the Viewing Tower, which commands one of the best viewpoints on the North Coast.

Giant's Causeway Visitor Centre

Causeway Road, Bushmills, Co Antrim
Tel: 028-20731582   Fax: 028-20732963
giantscauseway@nationaltrust.org.uk   www.nationaltrust.org.uk

- Open daily year round, 10.00 to 5.00 (later in summer)
- No entrance fee
- Located on B146 Causeway–Dunseverick road two miles from Bushmills
- Caters for school groups/tours

This famous geological phenomenon, renowned for its polygonal columns of layered basalt, is the only World Heritage Site in Ireland. Resulting from a volcanic eruption 60 million years ago, the Causeway is a designated Area of Outstanding Natural Beauty and has attracted visitors for centuries. It harbours a wealth of local and natural history that can be enjoyed from the North Antrim Coastal Path. The Centre has an education room and children's quiz/trail.

Irish Linen Centre and Lisburn Museum

Market Square, Lisburn, Co Antrim
Tel: 028-92663377   Fax: 028-92672624
ilcreception@lisburn.gov.uk

- Open Monday to Saturday, 9.30 to 5.00
- No entrance fee
- Located off the M1 at A49, ten miles
  from Belfast
- Caters for school groups/tours
- Special programmes for children

The Irish Linen Centre houses the permanent Flax to Fabric exhibition which tells the story of Irish linen from ancient times to the present day. The Lisburn Museum was founded to tell the story of the Lagan Valley area. Free tours are available if booked in advance, and workshops can be provided for children. Contact the Education Assistant for details.

Island Arts Centre

Lagan Valley Island, Lisburn, Co Antrim
Tel: 028-9250-9509   Fax: 028-9250-9510
arts.information@iac.lisburn.gov.uk   www.lisburncity.gov.uk

- Open Monday to Friday, 9.30 to 10.00, Saturday, 10.00 to
  5.00
- Free entrance; event and workshop prices on request
- Located on the banks of River Lagan at Lagan Valley Island
- Caters for children's parties
- Caters for school groups/tours
- Special programmes for children

Billed as the "Most Modern Arts Venue on the Island", the Island Arts Centre runs a year round first-class programme of diverse classes and workshops including visual and verbal arts, community arts, performing arts and a full education programme that actively encourages children to explore and preserve our arts heritage. Popular classes include After School Art Club, Kids 'n' Clay, The Culture Club and Mini Master. One-day workshops for kids are also available. An Arty Party, a birthday party with a difference, is available for kids of all ages.

Lagan Valley Leisureplex

12, Lisburn Leisure Park, Lisburn, Co Antrim
Tel: 028-92672121   Fax: 028-92674322
leisureplex@lisburn.gov.uk   www.lisburn.gov.uk

- Open Monday to Friday, 7.00 to 10.00; weekends, 9.00 to 5.30
- Costs vary per activity
- Located in Lisburn one mile from junction 7 off M1 motorway
- Caters for children's parties
- Caters for school groups/tours
- Special programmes for children
- 🍽 ♿ 🚻

The fun-packed leisure pool at the Lagan Valley Leisureplex includes the Lazy River Ride, Falling Rapids Ride, Drag Racer, Master Blaster, Rubber Ring Ride, Space Bowl, Sunken Pirate Galleon and Bubble Lounger. Birthday parties with bouncy castles, inflatable slides and Formula 1 racing cars are a specialty. For adults there is an eight-lane swimming pool and a complete health and fitness centre.

Larne Museum, Carnegie Centre and Arts

2 Victoria Road, Larne, Co Antrim
Tel: 028-287294821
www.larne.gov.uk

- Open Easter to August, Monday to Saturday, 12.30 to 5.00; September to Easter, Monday to Friday, 12.30 to 5.00
- Admission is free
- Located in the town centre of Larne
- Special programmes for children
- Caters for school groups/tours
- 🚻 ♿

The newly opened Carnegie Centre houses Larne Museum, a temporary exhibition gallery, auditorium and education centre. The museum charts Larne Borough's maritime, agricultural, industrial and social history through a range of exhibits and interactive features. The temporary gallery has a wide variety of exhibitions throughout the year, including historic costume and art exhibitions. The museum's education programme in 2006 included "Home Life in Larne during the Last Hundred Years" for Key Stage 1 pupils and "Children at Play in Victorian Times" for Key Stage 2 pupils.

Patterson's Spade Mill

Antrim Road, Templepatrick, Co Antrim
Tel: 028-94433619   Fax: 028-94433619
www.nationaltrust.org.uk

- Open daily June 1 to August 31, 2.00 to 6.00; April 1 to May 31 and September, open weekends, 2.00 to 6.00
- Adults, £3.90; Children, £2.30; Family, £10.10; Group, £3.30; Group out of hours, £5.20
- Located two miles NE of Templepatrick on Antrim—Belfast road
- Caters for school groups/tours

The last surviving water-driven spade mill in Ireland and popular with all ages. Hear and smell the grit on a guided tour of traditional spade-making, including the history and culture of the humble turf and garden spade. Visitors can purchase one of only 200 tailor-made spades made by hand every year. There are numerous hands-on activities and a children's guide is available.

TACT Wildlife Centre

Talnotry Avian Care Trust, 2 Crumlin Road, Crumlin, Co Antrim
Tel: 028-94422900   Fax: 028-94422900
t.a.c.t.@care4free.net   www.tactwildlifecentre.org.uk

- Open year round, Monday to Friday, 12.00 to 3.00; Sunday, 2.00 to 5.00 (or telephone to arrange a time)
- Adults, £3.00; Children, £2.00
- Located in the village of Crumlin
- Caters for children's parties
- Caters for school groups/tours

Located in a 200-year-old walled gardern, TACT Wildlife Centre is home to a wide variety of injured wildlife, including foxes, badgers, hares, rabbits, swans, owls, birds of prey, seabirds and many more. These animals are cared for in a natural environment and when possible are then returned to the wild after treatment. Children can hold a rabbit, feel a hedgehog's prickles or handle a bird of prey.

Ulster Museum

Botanic Gardens, Belfast
Tel: 028-90383000   Fax: 028-90383003
info@magni.org.uk   www.ulstermuseum.org.uk

- Open year-round Monday to Friday, 10.00 to 5.00; Saturday, 1.00 to 5.00; Sunday, 2.00 to 5.00
- No entrance fee
- Located in the Botanic Gardens, adjacent to Queen's University
- Caters for school groups/tours

Set in the Botanic Gardens in south Belfast, the Ulster Museum is Northern Ireland's treasure house of the past and present. Its collections are comprehensive and fascinating, covering fine and applied art, archaeology and ethnography, local history and natural sciences. A combination of permanent displays, temporary exhibitions and related events offers visitors the chance to enjoy a strong visual arts programme, discover the unfolding story of the north from the Ice Age to the twentieth century and explore the diversity of the country's natural history. [Note: Museum is planning to close for two years in autumn 2006 for major refurbishment]

Whowhatwherewhenwhy — W5

W5 at Odyssey, 2 Queen's Quay, Belfast
Tel: 028-90467700   Fax: 028-90467707
www.w5online.co.uk

- Open year round Monday to Saturday, 10.00 to 6.00; Sunday, 12.00 to 6.00
- Adults, £6.00; Children, £4.00; Family, £17.00
- Located in Belfast city centre
- Caters for school groups/tours

W5 is the first interactive discovery centre of its kind on the island of Ireland and is located at the Odyssey complex in Belfast. The centre offers an entertaining day out that will appeal to visitors of all ages. W5 is filled with 140 unique interactive exhibits, which offer hours of fun as visitors explore the WHO, WHAT, WHERE, WHEN AND WHY'S of the science of everyday life. Attractions include cool cloud rings, a giant race-track, wiggle sticks, boat building and a flying machine. Visitors can test their senses through music and sound with a laser harp, slap pipes and sound labs, design their own robots or beat the lie detector!

Ardress House

64 Ardress Road, Portadown, Co Armagh
Tel: 028-8784573   Fax: 028-38851236
ardress@ntrust.org.uk   www.nationaltrust.org.uk

- Open weekends April to Spetember, and bank holidays 2.00 to 6.00
- Adults, £3.40; Children, £1.80; Family, £8.60
- Located on Ardress Road five miles from Portadown

♿ 🚹🚺

House tours of this elegant seventeenth-century farmhouse include the Adam-style drawing-room, fine furniture and paintings. The farmyard, with traditional farm implements, is very popular with children. The attractive garden has woodland and riverside walks. There is a fantastic children's play area.

The Argory

Moy, Dungannon, Co Armagh
Tel: 028-87784753   Fax; 028-87789598
argory@nationaltrust.org.uk   www.nationaltrust.org.uk

- Grounds open May to September, 10.00 to 8.00 (until 4.00 rest of year); House open daily July to August, 12.00 to 6.00; June, Monday to Friday, 1.00 to 6.00; weekends, 12.00 to 6.00
- Tour: Adults, £4.70; Children, £2.50; Family, £11.90
- Located on Derrycaw Road, four miles from Moy
- Caters for school groups/tours

🍽 ♿ 🚹🚺 🎁

The Argory is a treasure trove, where the clock ticks but time stands still, and where nothing has been thrown away for 100 years. A guided tour takes visitors deep into this handsome Aladdin's Cave of Victorian and Edwardian tastes and interests. The Argory is built on a hill and has wonderful vistas over the gardens and 320-acre wooded riverside estate. Visitors can explore on foot using the way-marked trails along the River Blackwater or for the less energetic there is the Stable Yard to enjoy horse carriages, an acetylene gas plant and a cup of tea and award-winning scone.

Armagh County Museum

The Mall East, Armagh
Tel: 028-37523070

acm.info@magni.org.uk   www.armaghcountymuseum.org.uk

- Open Monday to Friday, 10.00 to 5.00; Saturday, 10.00 to 1.00, 2.00 to 5.00
- Admission is free
- Located on the Mall in Armagh
- Caters for school groups/tours
- Special programmes for children

The oldest county museum in Ireland, the extensive collections and displays reflect the lives of people who have lived and worked in Armagh or have been associated with the county. There are military uniforms, wedding dresses, ceramics, natural history specimens, railway memorabilia and an impressive art collection which includes works by many well-known Irish artists. In addition to the range of temporary exhibitions the museum offers a series of workshops based around the primary school curriculum. These take place in the museum and use objects and resources from the collections.

Armagh Planetarium

College Hill, Armagh
Tel: 048-37523689   Fax: 048-37526187
eamon@armaghplanet.com   www.armaghplanet.com

- Open Monday to Friday, 2.00 to 4.45
- Adults, £3.75; Children, £2.75; Family, £11.00
- Located on the Portadown Road in Armagh
- Caters for school groups/tours
- Special programmes for children

Armagh Planetarium offers a wide variety of educational activities for children. They can experience the wonders of the night sky inside the stardome inflatable planetarium. They can also look inside the telescope dome which houses the largest public telescope in Ireland. Please note that booking in advance is recommended for all visits to the Planetarium. [Note: Planetarium is closed for refurbishment until mid-2006; enquire for details.]

Gosford Forest Park

Gosford Demesne, Markethill, Armagh
Tel: 028-37551277   Fax: 028-37552143

- Open daily 8.00 to dusk
- Fees: £4.00 per car; Pedestrians: adults, £1.50, children, £0.50
- Located on the A28 from Newry to Armagh
- Caters for school groups/tours
- Special programmes for children

Gosford Forest Park comprises 240 hectares set in gently rolling drumlin country. Included on the grounds is an arboretum, wildfowl ponds, a collection of traditional species of poultry, an exhibition and lecture room, way-marked trails, the ruins of an old manor house and a nineteenth-century castle. Educational tours are available but must be pre-booked.

Millennium Court Arts Centre

William Street, Portadown, Co Armagh
Tel: 028-38394415
info@millenniumcourt.org   www.millenniumcourt.org

- Open Tuesday to Thursday, 10.00 to 9.00; Monday, Friday and Saturday, 10.00 to 5.00
- Admission is free
- Located in town centre just off Market Street
- Caters for school groups/tours

Millennium Court Arts Centre houses two purpose-built gallery spaces and has been described as one of Ireland's premier art spaces. Within the complex there is also a darkroom, visual arts workshop and artist-in-residence suite, all of which combine to create a vibrant and unique environment in which to cultivate and enhance the cultural environment of the community. The Millennium Court Arts Centre is committed to developing innovative education activities and projects for diverse audiences. During each exhibition the centre delivers a regular series of talks and events and specific outreach activities for schools and community groups.

Navan Centre and Fort

Navan Centre, Killylea Road, Armagh
Tel: 028-37521801   Fax: 028-37510180
navan@armagh.gov.uk   www.visitarmagh.com

Heritage**ISLAND**
IRELAND'S VISITOR ATTRACTIONS

- Open June to August, Monday to Saturday, 10.00 to 5.00; Sunday, 12.00 to 5.00; April to May and September, Saturday, 10.00 to 5.00, Sunday, 12.00 to 5.00
- Adults, £4.50; Children, £2.75; Family, £11.00
- Located off A28 west of Armagh
- Caters for school groups/tours
- ⦿ �

Navan Fort is a large earthwork of circular plan surrounding the summit of a drumlin in pleasant rolling countryside. The site, a pagan sanctuary, is some 240 metres in internal diameter. The impressive earthwork encloses two monuments on the hilltop, a ring barrow (Iron Age burial site) and a large mound. Excavations in the 1960s revealed that the mound was a composite structure built in 95 BC at the end of a long sequence of earlier activity. Recent excavations demonstrated that the main enclosure was also built in the 90s BC.

Palace Stables Heritage Centre

Palace Demesne, Armagh City
Tel: 028-37521801   Fax: 028-37520180
stables@armagh.gov.uk   www.visitarmagh.com

Heritage**ISLAND**
IRELAND'S VISITOR ATTRACTIONS

- Open June to August, Monday to Saturday, 10.00 to 5.00, Sunday, 12.00 to 5.00; April to May and September, Saturday, 10.00 to 5.00, Sunday, 12.00 to 5.00
- Adults, £4.50; Children, £2.75; Family, £11.00
- Located in the centre of Armagh
- Caters for children's parties
- Caters for school groups/tours
- Special programmes for children

⦿ ♿ ♂♀ 🎁

The Palace Stables Heritage Centre is a restored Georgian stable block in the Palace Demesne in the heart of Armagh city. Visitors can experience eighteenth-century life through a permanent exhibition, "A Day in the Life", living history interpreters who re-enact Georgian life in 1786, and guided tours of the Primate's Chapel and grounds. For children there is an extensive range of educational activities as well as a themed adventure play area set in mature woodland beside the car park.

Saint Patrick's Trian Visitor Complex

40 English Street, Armagh
Tel: 028-37521801   Fax: 028-37520180
info@saintpatrickstrian.com   www.visitarmagh.com

- Open Monday to Saturday, 10.00 to 5.00, Sunday, 2.00 to 5.00
- Adults, £4.50; Children, £2.75; Family, £11.00
- Located in the centre of Armagh
- Caters for children's parties
- Caters for school groups/tours
- Special programmes for children

Since the coming of Saint Patrick, Armagh has been steeped in religious history. Saint Patrick's Trian is the ideal place to discover Armagh's history, architecture, famous people and other sites of historical interest. The Visitors Centre incorporates three inspirational exhibitions under one roof: The Armagh Story, Saint Patrick's Testament and the Land of Lilliput.

Cavan County Museum

Virginia Road, Ballyjamesduff, Co Cavan
Tel: 049-8544070   Fax: 049-8544332
ccmuseum@eircom.net   www.cavanmuseum.ie

- Open year round, Tuesday to Saturday, 10.00 to 5.00; open Sundays June to October, 2.00 to 6.00
- Adults, €3.00; Children, €1.50; Family, €8.00
- Located just outside Ballyjamesduff
- Caters for school groups/tours

Cavan County Museum, a magnificent nineteenth-century building, provides visitors with an insight into the heritage of Cavan from antiquity to recent times. Rare and precious artefacts on display include the 4,000-year-old Killycluggin stone and three-faced Corleck Head. Also on display are the 1,000-year-old Lough Errol Log Boat, medieval Sheela-na-gigs, the eighteenth-century Cavan Mace, implements and machinery used by our ancestors, as well as interesting costume and sports galleries.

Introducing Children to Ecology

Dr Catherine O'Connell

Look up ecology in the dictionary and here's what it says: "Ecology is the study of living organisms and their habits in relation to their habitat." A child-friendly definition might be: "A study of all the plants and animals found in one place, the way they live and the things they need to survive."

Ecology begins in your back yard. It's like fitting together a jigsaw puzzle made of four pieces — plants, animals, environment and soil. Start your child off by marking out a four-metre square piece of the lawn (a grassland habitat). Then with notebook and pencil to one side, it's down on the hands and knees to look at the plants found there. Set a target. Find ten different plants and mosses in the lawn (for example, grass, daisy, dandelion, clover, self heal, moss and so on). Next try to determine how many of each of the ten plants on the list there are. For example, it could be one dandelion plant but over 100 grass plants. Everything goes into the notebook.

To make a list of ten animals is a bit trickier. It requires total adoration, so lie down flat with your nose in the grass and watch. Perhaps a fly will land for a few seconds before setting off again. An earwig might be seen crawling about in search of food. It will soon become obvious that ingenuity is needed to make a list of ten animals. This will bring you and your child into the area of making simple animal-friendly traps. So on a piece of the lawn turn a few old flower pots upside down, lay out a piece of damp carpet, some builders' bricks with holes, a piece of wood and leave them for about three weeks. You could also make a pitfall trap by digging a small hole in the lawn, lining it with a plastic cup with a small hole or crack in the bottom to allow for drainage and covering the top with a piece of board raised on two small rocks.

The animals you find in these traps fall into two groups. Generally the fast movers such as spiders, centipedes and ground beetles are carnivores and the slow-moving creatures such as slugs, snails and earthworms are herbivores. On the old wood you'll find wood lice and millipedes. A night-time safari with a torch will help the children realise that many of these creatures are nocturnal in habit. On rainy days encourage children to watch their habitat from the window to see if blackbirds or robins land in search of worms.

A little time can be spent in books trying to figure out what each creature eats and so the children are beginning to make food chains and see the links between the plants and animals in their habitat. You could leave part of the lawn to grow and see the differences you find.

Other pieces of the puzzle to be fit into the ecology study are environmental factors such as rainfall, temperature and sunlight and soil factors such as its content, moisture and aeration. A little ingenuity and you can design your own investigations to see the influence of these factors on the creatures and plants in the grassland habitat.

Another place where great ecology can be done is on summer holidays at the seashore, especially in rock pools. My own favourite habitat for ecology has to be the wet bogs. Now there's a wonderful puzzle to make!

Dr Catherine O'Connell is Chief Executive of the Irish Peatland Conservation Council, Bog of Allen Nature Centre, Lullymore, Rathangan, Co Kildare

Brunswick Superbowl

Brunswick Lane, Pennyburn, Co Derry
Tel: 028-71371999   Fax: 028-71269072
fun@brunswicksuperbowl.com

- Open daily 9.00 until late
- Costs vary depending on activity
- Located on Brunswick Lane in Pennyburn
- Caters for children's parties

🍽️ 🚻

Brunswick Superbowl has something for all the family. Their computerised ten-pin bowling lanes offer state-of-the-art bowling for absolutely everyone. For children they have ball walls along the side of the lanes to keep the balls on the right track. Also available for children is an Adventure Castle with a Super Freefall, all types of swings and obstacles in a maze of fun and activity. There are also video games, pool tables, karaoke and free face painting on the weekends.

Ervey Wood Country Park

Claudy, Co Derry
Tel: 028-77722074   Fax: 028-77766571
www.ehsni.gov.uk/places/parks

- Open year round
- No entrance fee
- Located 5.5 km NW of Claudy and 12 km SE of Derry

Ervey Wood Country Park extends for over one km on the northern side of the flanks and floor of the Burntollet Glen, with the Burntollet River running adjacent to its southern boundary. It includes two woodlands, Ervey wood and Tamnymore wood, separated by the Crunkin burn. Physical features include a number of small waterfalls and wet rock faces, as well as a series of high cliffs and a broad river flood plain. With a wide range of wildlife and plant communities, Ervey Wood Country Park provides a pleasant walk in all seasons, although it is at its best in spring with bluebell, wood sorrel and primrose providing a spectacular woodland carpet.

Green Lane Museum

Weaving Shed, Roe Valley Country Park, Livamady, Co Derry
Tel: 028-77760304
www.limavady.gov.uk

- Open daily, May to September, 1.00 to 5.00
- No entrance fee
- Located in the Roe Valley Country Park, one mile outside Limavady

  &♿ 👫

The Green Lane Museum explores the nineteenth- and twentieth-century rural heritages of the Roe Valley. On display are examples of local trades, life on the farm, and working in the kitchen. Also included is a feature on linen, one of the key stories along with hydro-electricity. The museum is an old weaving shed, one of the many listed remains of industrial heritage throughout the park. Local stories are enhanced through temporary exhibitions.

Ness Wood Country Park

Co Derry
Tel: 028-77722074   Fax: 027-77766571
www.ehsni.gov.uk/places/parks

- Open year round
- No entrance fee
- Located 4.5 km NW of Claudy and 13 km SE of Derry

Ness Wood Country Park comprises 50 hectares of mixed woodland known as Ness, Ervey and Tamnymore, in the sheltered Burntollet Valley. The main feature of the Park is a spectacular waterfall (the highest in the province) from which the Park derives its name, based on the Irish "an las" or Ness meaning waterfall. After the last ice age, 10,000 years ago, the old Burntollet River course was choked by glacial boulder clay deposits. In eroding a new channel through the underlying metamorphic schist rocks, the river has created the magnificent waterfall, gorges, potholes and rapids which are a feature of Ness Wood today.

Portstewart Strand

Portstewart, Co Derry
Tel: 028-70836396   Fax: 028-70836396
portstewart@nationaltrust.org.uk   www.nationaltrust.org.uk

- Access all year. Facilities open daily March to September, 10.00 to 6.00; October, weekends, 10.00 to 5.00
- Entrance fee: Car, £4.00; Minibus, £12.00
- Located a few minutes from the centre of Portstewart

The magnificent strand at Portstewart conjures up images of lazy summer days, picnics, sand castles and long walks. The two miles of yellow sand is one of Northern Ireland's finest beaches. A designated blue flag beach, it has designated no-car areas, a children's play area and water sports zone.

Riverwatch

Loughs Agency, 22 Victoria Road, Derry
Tel: 028-7134-2100   Fax: 028-7134-2720
gillian@loughs-agency.org   www.loughs-agency.org

- Open daily year round (except Bank Holidays), 10.00 to 4.00 (open evenings and weekends upon request)
- No entrance fee
- Located on the banks of the Foyle, one mile from Craigavon Bridge
- Caters for children's parties
- Caters for school groups/tours
- Special programmes for children
- ♿ ♀♂

Riverwatch is the Loughs Agency's Interpretative Centre. Its aim is to raise the awareness of the wonderful natural resources of Foyle and Carlingford Lough. Visitors will find unique exhibitions and displays that tell many stories about the life cycle of the salmon, angling, shellfish, the work of the Loughs Agency as well as four recently added aquarium tanks and more. Specific activities for children can be arranged in advance.

Roe Valley Country Park

41 Dogleap Road, Limavady, Co Derry
Tel: 028-77722074   Fax: 028-77766571
www.ehsni.gov.uk/places/parks

- Open daily, 9.00 to 6.00, April 1 to September 30; Monday to Friday, 9.00 to 5.00, October 1 to March 31
- No entrance fee
- Located off the B192 road outside of Limavady

Roe Valley Country Park runs for three miles either side of the River Roe near Limavady. The Park is the habitat of foxes, badgers and otters and over 60 species of bird have been seen. The Country Park contains a countryside museum and the Dogleap Centre where the story of the valley is told. The Centre also contains a café and an audio-visual theatre. There is even a disabled angler's jetty by the river. For the disabled visitor there is a specially designed trail emphasising the wildlife of the park. This includes an audio guide for blind and partially sighted visitors.

Springhill House and Costume Collection

20 Springhill Road, Moneymore, Co Derry
Tel: 028-86748210   Fax: 028-86748210
springhill@nationaltrust.org.uk   www.nationaltrust.org.uk

- Open daily July to August, 12.00 to 6.00; March 15 to June, September, weekends 12.00 to 6.00
- Adults, £4.30; Children, £2.30; Family, £10.90
- Located one mile from Moneymore on B18
- Caters for school groups/tours

Springhill has a beguiling spirit that has much to do with the lovely gardens, its simple but pretty "Plantation" house and 300 years of intriguing history. The guide will add to the mysterious allure with stories of the gentle ghost, Olivia. Visitors can also see the Costume Collection in the Laundry which is a stunning collection of colourful *haute couture* and day-to-day clothing and accessories with some pieces dating back to the seventeenth century. There are also beautiful walled gardens and a beech tree walk.

Tower Museum and La Trinidad Valencera

Union Hall Place, Derry
Tel: 028-71372411
www.derrycity.gov.uk/museums

Heritage ISLAND
IRELAND'S VISITOR ATTRACTIONS

- Open April to September, Monday to Saturday, 10.00 to 4.30; July to August, telephone for times on Sundays
- Admission: Adults, £3.00; Group/school rate, £2.50
- Located in the city centre opposite the Guildhall
- Caters for school groups/tours

The Tower Museum is the venue for a fascinating exhibition of an Armada shipwreck, *La Trinidad Valencera*, which puts on display many of the artefacts recovered from the sunken ship. This vessel was one of the largest ships in the Armada fleet and foundered in Kinnagoe Bay, just along the north coast of Donegal, during a violent storm in 1588. The excavation was one of the first underwater archaeological ventures of its kind and has supplied a stunning collection of material through revolutionary techniques invented to excavate, chart and recover the material from the ship.

Donegal Adventure Centre

Bayview Avenue, Bundoran, Co Donegal
Tel: 071-9842418   Fax: 071-9842429
info@donegal-holidays.com   www.donegal-holidays.com

- Open year round from 9.00 to dark
- Fees vary by activity
- Located in Bundoran
- Caters for children's parties
- Caters for school groups/tours
- Special programmes for children

At the Donegal Adventure Centre children benefit from being active, meet new friends, and learn to enjoy the outdoors safely. Among the activities at the Centre are surfing, kayaking, hillwalking, horse riding, cliff jumping, gorge walking, archery, rock climbing, abseiling, scuba diving and snorkelling.

Colmcille Heritage Centre
Letterkenny, Co Donegal
Tel: 074-9137306/7021/7044

- Open Easter week and early May to late September. Open for groups by appointment
- Adults, €2.00 (no charge for adults accompanying school groups); Students, €1.50
- Located in Gartan, Churchill, Letterkenny, off the L82 road
- Caters for school groups/tours
- Has special programmes for children

🍴 ♿ 👥 🎁

Situated on a lakeside 100-acre estate with nature walks, the centre features an exhibition on St Colmcille, with an audio-visual exhibition and tapestry display. St Colmcille or Columba is thought to have been born in Gartan, close to Lough Gartan in County Donegal in approximately 521 AD. St Colmcille founded the Irish monasteries at Glencolmcille and Kells before founding his monastery on Iona in 563 AD. It was from there that he brought Christianity to the North of England. The Book of Kells was produced from the monastery at Iona. The exhibition is housed in a beautiful stone building on the shores of Lough Gartan in the Derryveagh mountain range.

Donegal Castle
Donegal town
Tel: 073-22405   Fax: 073-22436
www.heritageireland.ie

- Open daily mid-March to end of October, 10.00 to 6.00
- Adults, €3.80; Children, €1.50; Family, €9.50
- Located in Donegal town

👥

Built by the O'Donnell chieftain in the fifteenth century, beside the River Eske, the Castle has extensive seventeenth-century additions by Sir Basil Brooke. The Castle is furnished throughout and includes Persian rugs and French tapestries. Information panels chronicle the history of the Castle owners from the O'Donnell chieftains to the Brooke family. Limited access for people with disabilities to the ground floor. *An OPW site.*

Donegal County Museum

High Road, Letterkenny, Co Donegal
Tel: 074-9124613   Fax: 074-9126522
museum@donegalcoco.ie

Heritage**ISLAND**
IRELAND'S VISITOR ATTRACTIONS

- Open year round, Monday to Friday, 10.00 to 4.30; Saturday, 1.00 to 4.30
- No entrance fee
- Located across from the Revenue Office
  ♿ ♂♀

Donegal County Museum was first opened to the public in 1987 and is housed in what was once the Warden's house of the Letterkenny Workhouse, which was built in 1843. The role of Donegal County Museum is to collect, record, preserve, communicate and display for the use and enjoyment of the widest community possible, the material evidence and associated information of the history of Donegal. The Museum holds a substantial collection of original artefacts representing the history of Co Donegal and covering subjects such as archaeology, history, social history and folklife.

Glebe House and Gallery
(The Derek Hill Collection)

Churchill, Letterkenny, Co Donegal
Tel: 074-9137071
www.heritageireland.ie

- Open mid-May to September, Saturday to Thursday, 11.00 to 6.30
- Adults, €2.90; Children, €1.30; Family, €7.40
- Located 18 km from Letterkenny on R251

  🍽 ♿ ♂♀

The Glebe House and Gallery is situated in a Regency House, built in 1828, set in woodland gardens, decorated with William Morris textiles, Islamic and Japanese art, etc. The collection includes 300 works by leading twentieth-century artists — Picasso, Kokoshka as well as Irish and Italian artists. Exhibitions are shown in the adjoining gallery. Access to ground floor of the Gallery for people with disabilities. *An OPW site.*

Glenveagh Castle and
Glenveagh National Park

Churchill, Letterkenny, Co Donegal
Tel: 074-9137090   Fax: 074-9137072
www.heritageireland.ie

- Open daily mid-March to early November, 10.00 to 6.30
- Adults, €2.90 Children, €1.30; Family, €7.40
- Located 24 km NW of Letterkenny

🍽 ♿ 🚻

Built in the years 1870-1873, Glenveagh Castle consists of a four-storey rectangular keep. Access to the interior is by tour only. The castle is surrounded by one of the finest gardens in Ireland, which contrasts with the rugged surroundings. Glenveagh National Park includes 16,540 hectares (40,873 acres) of mountains, lakes, glens and woods, with a herd of red deer. The Visitor Centre includes displays explaining the Park along with an audio-visual show. Visitor Centre is accessible for people with disabilities. *An OPW site.*

Ionad Cois Locha

Dunlewey Centre, Gweedore, Letterkenny, Co Donegal
Tel: 074-9531699   Fax: 074-9531968
dunleweycentre@eircom.net   www.dunleweycentre.com

- Open from March 17 to November 2, Monday to Saturday, 10.30 to 6.00, Sunday, 11.00 to 6.00
- Located ten km from Gweedore
- Contact Ionad Cois Locha for admission rates
- Caters for children's parties
- Caters for school groups/tours
- Special programmes for children

🍽 ♿ 🚻 🎁

Ionad Cois Locha is a community co-operative project located in an Irish-speaking area in Donegal. Situated on the shores of Dunlewey Lough in the shadow of the haunting and mysterious Poison Glen, facilities at Ionad Cois Locha include a visitors centre, demonstrations of carding, spinning and weaving wool, a play area, story-telling, boat trips on Dunlewey Lake and a craft shop and museum. Special school tour rates are available.

Jungle King Play Centre

Oldtown, Letterkenny, Co Donegal
Tel: 074-9177731
www.jungleking.ie

- Open daily 10.00 to 7.00
- Admission, €7.00
- Located in Oldtown, Letterkenny
- Caters for children's parties

🍽 👫

Jungle King Play Centre is a state of the art children's indoor activity centre for children up to twelve years old. There is a separate area for babies with soft padded animals and a ball pool. Under fours can play in a two-level climbing frame. For five- to twelve-year-olds there is a large frame which includes a three-lane astra slide, spiral slide, rope bridges and football court. The centre has a comfortable coffee dock for parents to relax.

Leisureland Redcastle

Moville, Co Donegal
Tel: 074-9382306   Fax: 074-9382306

- Open daily in summer from 12.00 to 6.00; open weekends from March 1 to October 31
- No entrance fee, costs vary depending on activity
- Caters for children's parties
- Caters for school groups/tours

🍽 ♿ 👫 🎁

Leisureland Redcastle is Ireland's largest indoor heated amusement centre catering for children of all ages. A new three-level adventure play system has been added, plus Circus Carousel, Safari Train, Dodgems, Small Car Track, Pirate Ship, Aqua Blasta Fire Station, Air Hockey, Ball Pool and much more.

Newmills Corn and Flax Mills

Churchill Road, Letterkenny, Co Donegal
Tel: 074-9125115
www.heritageireland.com

- Open daily mid-June to end of
  September, 10.00 to 6.30
- Adults, €2.90; Children, €1.30;
  Family, €7.40
- Located 5 km outside of Letterkenny
- ♿ ♟

The oldest surviving building here is said to be 400 years old. Indeed, the whole complex is an interesting reminder of a stage in the industrial development of this country which has now given way to a more sophisticated, but usually far less fascinating, technology. The visitor to Newmills can experience the pleasure of seeing one of the largest waterwheels in Ireland in action as it drives the machinery of the corn mill. *An OPW site.*

Waterworld

Seafront, Bundoran, Co Donegal
Tel: 071-9841172   Fax: 071-9842168
info@waterwoldbundoran.com   www.waterworldbundoran.com

- Open daily June to August, 10.00 to
  7.00; weekends in May and September,
  10.00 to 7.00
- Contact Waterworld for admission costs
- Located at seafront in Bundoran
- Caters for children's parties
- Caters for school groups/tours
- ♟ ♿ ♟ 🎁

Waterworld in Bundoran offers indoor adventure for the whole family. Facilities include a Wave Pool, Slide Pool, Rapids, Tornado Flume, beach area, children's play featues and the Whizzer, the fastest water slide in Ireland (65 metres long, 50-step high tower, 9.5 degree incline and aquacatch landing). For the adults there are also steam cabinets, sea baths, a sunbed and Relaxarium.

The Workhouse

Dunfanaghy, Co Donegal
Tel: 074-9136540
workhousedunfanaghy@eircom.net

- Open Easter to mid-September; other times by arrangement
- Adults, €4.25; Students/OAP, €3.00; Children, €2.00
- Located on the N56 in Figart, in west Dunfanaghy village
- Caters for school groups/tours
- Has special programmes for children

This comprehensive exhibition illustrates the era of the Great Famine by way of models and a series of tableaux telling the true story of one survivor. It also houses an ecological exhibition on landscape and archaeology and offers a wildlife-friendly garden, art gallery and book shop. Contact for details of workshops and activities for children.

Ballycopeland Windmill

near Millisle, Co Down
028-90546552 (Environment and Heritage Service)
www.ehsni.gov.uk/places/monuments

- Open July and August, Wednesday and Thursday 10.00 to 1.00; Tuesday, Friday, Saturday and Sunday 2.00 to 6.00
- No entrance fee
- Located one mile west of Millisle village centre on the B172

Restored to full working order, this late-eighteenth-century corn mill, for flour and animal feed, with its miller's house and associated buildings, gives a unique insight into a lost industry. Much to the amusement of younger visitors, a large wooden pig greets visitors before they enter the kiln house. Inside the kiln house there is a video explaining how the mill works. There may also be a chance to mill some barley. The miller's house is also open with its impressive kitchen and fireplace containing a unique double flue. The outbuildings now serve as visitor centre with displays, models and audio-visual theatre.

Castle Ward

Strangford, Co Down
Tel: 028-4488-1204   Fax: 028-4488-1729
castleward@nationaltrust.org.uk   www.nationaltrust.org.uk   **H**eritage**ISLAND**
IRELAND'S VISITOR ATTRACTIONS

- Open daily July to August, 1.00 to 6.00; contact for times rest of year
- Grounds, Wildlife Centre and House Tour: Adults, £5.50; Children, £2.50; Family, £13.50
- Located 1.5 miles from Strangford on the Downpatrick Road
- Caters for school groups/tours

⦿ ♿ ♟ 🎁

Superb Georgian house with both Classical and Gothic façades and interiors set in a 750-acre estate with breathtaking views over Strangford Lough. Several delightful walks to choose from ranging in duration from half an hour to three hours, through mature parklands, woodlands and lough shore areas. Of particular note are the Temple Water, a man-made pleasure lake and the old farm yard with seventeenth-century keep. There is also a Victorian pastimes centre and a children's playground.

Crawfordsburn Country Park

Bridge Road South, Helen's Bay, Co Down
Tel: 028-91853621   Fax: 028-91852580
www.ehsni.gov.uk/places/monuments

- Open daily April 1 to September 30, 9.00 to 8.00; October 1 to March 31, 9.00 to 4.45
- Contact park for entrance fee
- Located off A2 towards Bangor

Crawfordsburn Country Park is situated on the southern shores of Belfast Lough. It is full of variety, featuring 3.5 km of coastline, often rugged and rocky, the two best beaches in the Belfast area, a deep wooded glen with an impressive waterfall at its head, a pond and wildflower meadows with excellent views over the Lough. The Park also includes Grey Point Fort, a coastal battery and gun emplacement dating from early this century and updated during World War II. Visitors can also go to the Countryside Centre to see the exhibition "Choices in the Environment" which features a number of interactive displays.

Delamont Country Park

Mullagh, Killyleagh, Co Down
Tel: 028-44828333   Fax: 028-44828333
info@delamontcountrypark.com   www.delamontcountrypark.com

- Open daily 9.00 to dusk
- Fee for miniature railway: Adults,
  £2.50; Children, £1.50
- Located on the A22 on the main DPK
  to Comber Road
- Caters for children's parties
- Caters for school groups/tours
- Special programmes for children

Delamont Country Park is home to the longest miniature railway in Ireland as well as the Strangford Stone, which is the tallest megalith in Ireland. Situated on the Strangford Lough, the park offers stunning views and a relaxing atmosphere. Events and facilities include magic shows, Punch and Judy shows, model aircraft displays, forest walks, cruises on Strangford Lough, falcon displays, teddy bears' picnic and an outdoor adventure playground.

Down County Museum

The Mall, Downpatrick, Co Down
Tel: 028-44615218   Fax: 028-44615590
museum@downdc.gov.uk   www.downcountymuseum.com

HeritageISLAND
IRELAND'S VISITOR ATTRACTIONS

- Open Monday to Friday, 10.00 to 5.00;
  Saturday and Sunday, 1.00 to 5.00
- No entrance fee
- Located on the Mall, English Street,
  Downpatrick

Down County Museum, which is located in the historic buildings of the eighteenth-century County Gaol, collects, conserves and exhibits artefacts relating to the history of County Down from the earliest times until today. Its aim is to enhance appreciation of the history, culture and environment of the county through the organisation of exhibitions, activities and events which are informative, accessible and relevant to the local community and visitors.

Downpatrick and County Down Railway

Market Street, Downpatrick, Co Down
Tel: 028-44615779
downtrains@yahoo.co.uk   www.downrail.co.uk

- Open St Patrick's Day, Easter, May Day, summer weekends, last October weekend and first three December weekends
- Fares: Adults, £4.50; Children, £3.50; Family, £15.00
- Located on the Downpatrick—Newcastle Road, beside Bus Station

🍽 ♿ 👫 🎁

This railway is Northern Ireland's only standard gauge (i.e. full-size) heritage railway and is based in the county town of Down. The railway connects various sites of Down's Christian heritage, such as Inch Abbey and a grave of a Viking King, Magnus Barefoot. There are special trains on St Patrick's Day, Easter, a Hallowe'en Ghost Train and Santa Specials in December.

Dundrum Castle

Dundrum Village, Co Down
Tel: 028-90546518
www.ehsni.gov.uk/places/monuments

- Open April 1 to September 30, Tuesday to Saturday, 10.00 to 7.00; Sunday, 2.00 to 7.00; open October 1 to March 31, Saturday, 10.00 to 4.00; Sunday, 2.00 to 4.00
- No entrance fee
- Located in Dundrum village

👫

This medieval coastal castle with circular keep and massive walls is set high on a hill overlooking the sea. It was built shortly before 1210, on an earlier fortified earthwork, from which the place-name element "dun" derives. It was begun by John de Courcy, who led the 1177 Anglo-Norman invasion of East Ulster. Its purpose was to guard the land routes from Drogheda via Greencastle to Downpatrick. There are other sites linked with John de Courcy, the most important of which are Cathedral Hill and Mound of Down, both at Downpatrick, and the castles at Carrickfergus and Inch Abbey.

Exploris Aquarium

The Rope Walk, Castle Street, Portaferry, Co Down
Tel: 028-42728062   Fax: 028-42728396
william.rankin@ards-council.gov.uk   www.exploris.org.uk

- Open Monday to Friday, 10.00 to 6.00;
  Saturday, 11.00 to 6.00; Sunday, 1.00 to
  6.00 (closes one hour earlier September to
  March)
- Fees (peak season): Adults, £6.70; Children,
  £3.80; Family, £18.00
- Located in centre of Portaferry town
- Caters for school groups/tours

Exploris Aquarium is located in the conservation village of Portaferry, on the shores of Strangford Lough. Visitors can go on a journey from Strangford Lough out into the Irish Sea and experience fascinating creatures including octopus, majestic rays, six-foot-long conger eels, stingrays and shark species. Features include Touch Tank, Open Sea Tank, Fish Feeding and Marine Discovery Labs. In the NIE Seal Sanctuary visitors can see at close quarters the rehabilitation of sick or orphaned seals.

Grey Abbey

Strangford Lough, Co Down
Tel: 028-90546552 (Environment and Heritage Service)
www.ehsni.gov.uk/places/monuments

- Open April 1 to September 30, Tuesday to
  Saturday, 10.00 to 7.00, Sunday, 2.00 to
  7.00; October 1 to March 31, Saturday,
  10.00 to 4.00; Sunday, 2.00 to 4.00
- No entrance fee
- Located in Church Street, Greyabbey

These splendid ruins of a Cistercian abbey church and buildings are the finest example of Anglo-Norman ecclesiastical architecture in Northern Ireland. One of the great features of Grey Abbey today is a carefully recreated Herb Garden, containing over 50 varieties of medicinal plants and herbs that visitors are free to stroll through. The Abbey is set in the beautiful landscaped parkland of eighteenth-century Rosemount House but visitors should note that these grounds are private and should only wander among the ruins and the lawns.

Hillsborough Courthouse

The Square, Hillsborough, Co Down
Tel: 028-92689717
www.ehsni.gov.uk/places/monuments

- Open year round Monday to Saturday, 9.00 to 5.30; open Sundays, 2.00 to 6.00 in July and August
- No entrance fee
- Located in Hillsborough town centre

♟ ♟

This splendid Georgian market house was built c. 1760 in classical style, in a market square, as a focus within the planned development of Hillsborough. It was also used as a Courthouse from 1810, and the court room is still an evocative feature. There is an exhibition showing courtroom proceedings through the ages. The building is now used for exhibitions and functions and is home to Lisburn Borough Council Tourist Information Centre. Hillsborough Fort is nearby, approached through wrought iron gates, across the square from the courthouse.

Inch Abbey

Downpatrick, Co Down
028-90546552 (Environment and Heritage Service)
www.ehsni.gov.uk/places/monuments

- Open year round
- No entrance fee
- Located off the main Belfast-Downpatrick road, about 0.75 miles from Downpatrick

These extensive remains are of a Cistercian Abbey founded in 1180 by John de Courcy, who led the 1177 Anglo-Norman invasion of East Ulster. It is set in a beautiful location beside the River Quoile, with distant views towards de Courcy's Cathedral town of Downpatrick. De Courcy's wife, Affreca, founded Grey Abbey, also a Cistercian house. There are other sites linked with John de Courcy, the most important of which are Cathedral Hill and Mound of Down, both at Downpatrick, and the castles at Carrickfergus, Dundrum and Inch Abbey.

Jordan's Castle

Ardlgass, Co Down
Tel: 028-90546552
www.ehsni.gov.uk/places/monuments

- Open July and August, Tuesday, Friday and Saturday, 10.00 to 1.00; Wednesday and Thursday 2.00 to 6.00
- No entrance fee
- Located on the seafront overlooking the harbour and south of the marina

This fine preserved tower-house was built for a fifteenth-century merchant in Ardglass, County Down. Ardglass was an important port and town in the Anglo-Norman Earldom of Ulster and an impressive group of tower-houses are features of its townscape. Jordan's Castle is the best-preserved example. It was bought by the antiquarian Francis Joseph Bigger in 1911, who restored and furnished it. Thankfully he bequeathed it to the state in 1926 so that visitors can enjoy it today.

Mount Stewart House and Gardens

Near Greyabbey, Newtownards, Co Down
Tel: 028-42788387 Fax: 028-42788569
mountstewart@nationaltrust.org.uk
www.nationaltrust.org.uk

HeritageISLAND
IRELAND'S VISITOR ATTRACTIONS

- House open daily July to August, 12.00 to 6.00; ring for times rest of year
- Adults, £5.50; Children, £2.80; Family, £13.80 (reduced fees for Gardens only)
- Located five miles from Newtowards on Portaferry Road (A20)

Mount Stewart House, home of Lord Castlereagh, is a fascinating eighteenth-century house with nineteenth-century additions. It also has one of the great gardens in Ireland, largely created by the wife of the Seventh Marquis of Londonderry, with an unrivalled collection of rare and unusual plants, colourful parterres and magnificent formal and informal vistas. The Temple of the Winds, James "Athenian" Stuart's banqueting hall of 1785, overlooks Strangford Lough.

Nendrum Monastery

Mahee Island, Strangford Lough, Co Down
Tel: 028-90546552 (Environment and Heritage Service)
www.ehsni.gov.uk/places/monuments

- Open April 1 to September 30, Tuesday to Saturday, 10.00 to 7.00, Sunday, 2.00 to 7.00 (closes at 4.00 in winter)
- No entrance fee
- Located on Mahee Island in Strangford Lough, signposted off the A22 immediately south of Comber

👤👤

This fine example of an island monastery was traditionally founded in the fifth century by St Machaoi. The monastery comprises three concentric dry-stone walled enclosures with evidence of industrial work outside, including a tidal mill and landing places. The central enclosure has a church ruin with sundial, the remains of a round tower and a graveyard. A summer cottage and its driveway, built on the site in the early twentieth century, has been retained for use as a visitor centre. The Centre houses interactive and graphic displays, models, artefacts and video.

Quoile Countryside Centre

5 Quay Road, Downpatrick
Tel: 028-44615520   Fax: 028-44613280
www.ehsni.gov.uk/places/parks

- Visitors Centre open daily April 1 to August 31, 11.00 to 5.00; from September 1 to March 31, weekends, 1.00 to 5.00
- No entrance fee
- Located just off the A25 on road to Strangford

♿ 👤👤

The Quoile Pondage National Nature Reserve is situated just outside Downpatrick on either side of the Quoile River. The Pondage was created in 1957 by the construction of a tidal barrier to prevent flooding in the Downpatrick area. Today there is a diversity of habitat and wildlife that make the Quoile a great location to visit. Facilities at the reserve include the Quoile Countryside Centre with displays on the wildlife and history of the area. Situated on the Castle Island Road, a few minutes' drive from the Countryside Centre, is the Castle Island Bird-Watching Hide for excellent bird-watching. This distinctive hide comfortably seats 20 adults or 30 children, and is fully accessible for people with disabilities.

Redburn Country Park

Bangor, Co Down
Tel: 028-91811491   Fax: 028-91820695
www.ehsni.gov.uk/places/parks

- Open year round
- No entrance fee
- Located on Old Holywood Road near
  Palace Army Barracks

Redburn Country Park is set on an escarpment overlooking Belfast Lough. It includes the mature beech woods and the scrub and grasslands at the top of the hill. A dense canopy of beech wood provides good shelter for many of our more common birds such as tits and finches, while in summer, willow warbler and blackcaps may be found in the scrub and gorse at the top of the hill. Mammals too are plentiful with rabbits grazing in the open glades; and visitors may be lucky to catch a fleeting glimpse of the Park's shyest resident, the Red Squirrel.

Rowallane Garden

Saintfield, Co Down
Tel: 028-97510131   Fax: 028-97511242
uroest@smtp.nationaltrust.org.uk   www.nationaltrust.org.uk

- Open May to September, 10.00 to 8.00;
  October to April, 10.00 to 4.00
- Adults, £3.80; Children, £1.80; Family, £9.40
- Located on A7 one mile from Saintfield

Rowallane Gardens are a paradise for anyone who loves trees, greenery and a natural wilderness. Whether a plantsman, a rambler or a ten-year-old wanting to play hide and seek, visitors will enjoy the unexpected variety, the peace and the beautiful colours. It is an enchanting 52-acre garden that has been growing since the 1860s with many unusual trees, shrubs and other plants introduced from many parts of the world in the early 1900s. Planting and collecting continues today. Rowallane is a haven for all seasons and for all ages.

An Unsung Hero

Darina Shouldice

Webster's Third Dictionary defines a hero as "a man admired for his noble qualities and considered a model or ideal". I met a hero once. His life touched mine briefly some years ago and I'll never forget him.

I had taught Frank's son, Eric, for two years and had been struck by the child's exceptional gifts in all areas of the arts curriculum — creative writing, arts and crafts, music and drama. At a parent-teacher meeting Frank revealed his own interest in these areas, which he greatly enjoyed sharing with his children. Eric's creative confidence was easily understood when I heard how he and his dad would work out storylines together just for fun and illustrate them with imaginative cartoons; and how they would dramatise their work and practise interesting voices for the colourful characters they had conjured together.

On Saturday mornings their home — in a "low income" area of suburban Dublin — would host an art session for family and friends where the only limit on creative exploration was the limit of the imagination! At a time when many children are left to their electronic toys for company and entertainment, this was a rare and noteworthy collaboration.

Freshly inspired, I decided to expose my own young sons to a cultural treat one weekend. I had read about the Family Programme in the National Gallery where an open art session was offered free of charge to the general public every Saturday afternoon. As we sat on the floor of the Baroque Gallery in the shadow of a masterpiece, surrounded by hungry creative souls of every age, I felt a great sense of privilege. Squatting on cushions in auspicious surroundings, pencil and crayons in hand, adults became children again as they and their children became *artists* together. I thought of my "other" children in "disadvantaged" Dublin who were clearly not represented in the group for no apparent reason — admission was free and all materials were supplied — and I suddenly felt their cultural isolation.

As I scanned the room wondering whether I might know anyone here, my eyes came to rest on a familiar face which I couldn't place out of context. Moments later I saw a delighted Eric, his little brothers Gavin and Emmet and a cousin waving enthusiastically at me across the Great Hall. I felt a wave of emotion, including a mix of admiration, gratitude and humility. Admiration for the father who was so effectively guiding the creative journey of his young family; gratitude for his wholehearted support of their emerging creativity; and humility for the personal effort required of this man to move the experience of his children beyond the limits of their physical and social environment. I later learned that their trip to the National Art Gallery had been made every Saturday of the Family Programme and involved taking two buses, followed by a trek across town to Merrion Square with four little boys under eight. A heroic endeavour indeed!

After the art session we explored the Gallery together and then adjourned to the playground in Merrion Square. We spoke at length about the possibilities of expanding a child's creative vision by tapping into the resources that are freely available to all in the form of art galleries and museums. We spoke of fostering a vision of a better world for our children and of enriching their lives by exposing them early and often to the arts. We discussed why this experience is not more commonly shared by the community they live in.

That day and that conversation have stayed with me, partly because it proved to me the difference a person of vision can make in the life experience of a child; partly because it challenged an assumption I had made about cultural isolation; but mainly because Frank died in tragic circumstances not long after.

I felt devastated for the loss of this great man to his children, to his partner and family, and to his community which so desperately needs its heroes. But I took comfort from the knowledge that while his own light was extinguished prematurely, the light of curiosity, confidence and creativity that he lit in his children and others continues to shine and enrich their experience of life, and will continue on in their children, and their children's children. A noble and priceless legacy.

Darina Shouldice teaches in the junior school at OLI Darndale.

The Saint Patrick Centre

Downpatrick, Co Down
Tel: 028-44619000   Fax: 028-44619111
director@saintpatrickcentre.com   www.saintpatrickcentre.com

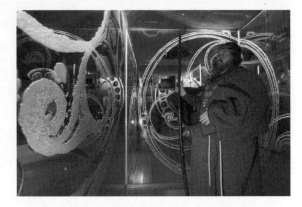

- Open April to September, Monday to Saturday, 9.30 to 6.30; Sunday, 1.00 to 5.30 (closes 30 minutes later in summer); October to March, Monday to Saturday, 10.00 to 5.00; St Patrick's Day, 9.30 to 7.00
- Adults, £4.90; Children, £2.50
- Located at foot of Cathedral Hill, traditional burial site of St Patrick
- Caters for school groups/tours

The Saint Patrick Centre is one of Northern Ireland's major Millennium Projects, housing the first permanent exhibition to tell the story of Ireland's patron saint. The exhibition, entitled "Ego Patricius", presents Patrick's story in his own words and in the context of the period. The exhibition uses state-of-the-art interpretation that gives visitors a real understanding of the arrival and establishment of Christianity in Ireland. Appropriately, the Centre is located in a stunning new building below the reputed burial site of St Patrick.

Scrabo Country Park

203A Scrabo Road, Newtownards
Tel: 028-91811491   Fax: 028-91820695
www.ehsni.gov.uk/places/parks

- Park open year round. Scrabo Tower open March to September, Saturday to Thursday 10.30 to 6.00
- No entrance fee
- Located off the A20 and A21

Scrabo Country Park is centred upon the tower built on the summit of Scrabo Hill. It includes the woodlands of Killynether, the disused quarries where Scrabo stone was once quarried, a pond and a prehistoric hill fort with adjacent enclosures and hut-circles. A wide range of bird life can also be observed in the park. A ten-minute audio-visual show, "Ebb and Flow", has been installed in a display on the upper floor of Scrabo tower. It tells the story of Strangford Lough and its wildlife.

The Somme Heritage Centre

233 Bangor Road, Newtownards, Co Down
Tel: 028-91823202   Fax: 028-91823214
sommeassociation@dnet.co.uk   www.irishsoldier.org

Heritage ISLAND
IRELAND'S VISITOR ATTRACTIONS

- Open July to August, Monday to Friday, 10.00 to 5.00, weekends, 12.00 to 5.00; September to June, Monday to Thursday, 10.00 to 4.00 (open Saturdays, 12.00 to 4.00 April to June, September)
- Adults, £3.75; Children, £2.75
- Located on the Bangor to Newtownards road
- Caters for school groups/tours

The Somme Heritage Centre examines Ireland's role in the First World War with special reference to the three volunteer divisions which comprised volunteers from both religions and traditions. During guided tours the visitor is taken back through a "time-tunnel" to Ireland in 1910 and learns about the Home Rule Crisis, the backdrop to Ireland's involvement in the War. The highlight of the Centre is a recreated front-line trench, from which visitors can look out over "No Man's Land" and view a dramatic audio-visual narrative of the Somme battle.

Ulster Folk and Transport Museum

Cultra, Holywood, Co Down
Tel: 028-90428428   Fax: 028-90428728
www.uftm.org.uk

Heritage ISLAND
IRELAND'S VISITOR ATTRACTIONS

- Open daily July to September, 10.00 to 6.00, Sunday, 11.00 to 6.00; October to February, Monday to Friday, 10.00 to 4.00; March to June, Monday to Friday, 10.00 to 5.00; Saturday, 10.00 to 6.00; Sunday, 11.00 to 6.00
- Adults, £6.50; Children, £3.50; Family, £18.00
- Located on the main Belfast to Bangor Road
- Caters for school groups/tours
- Special programmes for children

Visitors to the Museum take a journey into the past to cottages and prosperous farms to learn about the daily lives of the inhabitants. Various buildings have been painstakingly removed from their original sites and re-erected at the Museum. Exhibitions include the Irish Railway Collection, The Flight Experience, Road Transport, Meet the Victorians, demonstrations of lace making, sampler making, spinning, weaving, wood turning, open hearth cooking, basket making and needlework.

Belleek Pottery Visitor Centre

Belleek, Co Fermanagh
Tel: 028-68658501   Fax: 028-68658625
visitorcentre@belleek.ie   www.belleek.ie

HeritageISLAND
IRELAND'S VISITOR ATTRACTIONS

- Open July to September, Monday to Friday,
  9.00 to 6.00; Saturday, 10.00 to 6.00;
  Sunday, 2.00 to 6.00; contact for times rest
  of year
- Adults, £4.00; Children, free
- Located in Belleek Town
- Caters for school groups/tours

At Belleek Pottery, the methods and techniques developed by the very first craftsmen are still followed today. Visitors will learn how the intricate strands of the basketware are woven together using techniques passed down from generation to generation. They will see how tiny petals, stems and twigs are created by hand and discover the secret that gives Belleek Parian China its distinctive pearly glow. The tour then passes through to the furnace area and ends in the painting rooms where the delicate colours of nature are artfully applied.

Castle Archdale Country Park

Irvinestown, Co Fermanagh
Tel: 028-68621588   Fax: 028-68621375
www.ehsni.gov.uk/places/monuments

- Museum and Visitor Centre open July 1 to
  August 31, Tuesday to Sunday, 11.00 to 7.00;
  open from Easter to June 30, Sundays, 12.00
  to 6.00
- Contact Park for entrance fee details
- Located on the Enniskillen to Kesh road (A32)

Castle Archdale Country Park cover 230 acres along the shores of Lower Lough Erne. Castle Archdale is based on the demesne of the Archdale Manor House, which was built in 1773, of which now only the courtyard buildings remain. Features within the Park include a red deer enclosure, wildfowl ponds, nature trail, butterfly garden and wildflower meadow. Evidence of the 1939—45 War can also be found throughout the park in flying-boat docks, ammunition dumps, slit trenches, etc. Castle Archdale was the main base from which they flew and this is highlighted in an exhibition within the Centre entitled "Castle Archdale at War".

Castle Coole

Enniskillen, Co Fermanagh
Tel: 028-66322690   Fax: 028-66325665
castlecoole@nationaltrust.org.uk   www.nationaltrust.org.uk

- Grounds open April to October, 10.00 to 8.00; November to March, 10.00 to 4.00; House open daily July to August, 12.00 to 6.00
- Grounds and House tours, Adults, £4.50; Children, £2.00; Family, £11.00
- Located on the A2 one mile from Enniskillen
- Caters for school groups/tours

Located on the edge of Enniskillen, Castle Coole is one of the treasures of the National Trust. Designed by James Wyatt and completed in 1798 for the first Earl of Belmore, Castle Coole's interior was created by some of the leading craftsmen of the eighteenth century. The surrounding 700-acre estate is a fitting setting for the mansion with parkland, Lough Coole and extensive woods. Visitors can also enjoy walks through The Grand Yard, Servants Quarters, Ice House and view the original Belmore Coach.

Crom Estate Visitors Centre

Newtownbutler, Co Fermanagh
Tel: 028-67738118   Fax: 028-67738118
crom@nationaltrust.org.uk   www.nationaltrust.org.uk

- Grounds open daily mid-March to mid-October (hours vary); Visitors centre open 10.00 to 6.00, weekends from mid-March and daily from mid-April, to September
- Fees: £4.80 per car/boat
- Located three miles from Newtownbutler
- Caters for children's parties
- Caters for school groups/tours

Crom Estate, run by the National Trust, is one of the most important nature conservation sites in Ireland. Located on the tranquil shores of Lough Erne, Crom can be reached by either car or boat. At the Visitors Centre is an interpretation centre on the history and wildlife of Crom, boats for hire, passes for pike and coarse fishing and a children's play area.

Devenish Monastic Site

Enniskillen, Co Fermanagh
Tel: 028-68621588
www.ehsni.gov.uk/places/monuments

- Open daily April 1 to September 30 (ferry runs from Easter to mid-September)
- Cost of ferry to island: Adults, £2.25; Children, £1.20
- Ferry leaves from Trory point, at the junction of the B52 to Kesh and the A32 to Ballinamallard, 1.5 miles out of Enniskillen.

♦♦

This site contains the substantial remains of Lough Erne's most important island monastery. The remains include a Romanesque church and a twelfthcentury round tower, crosses and the Priory Church. Visitors can climb the island's most striking feature, the perfect round tower, which is 30 metres tall. There is also a museum which contains sculpture from the churches.

Enniskillen Castle and Museums

Castle Barracks, Enniskillen, Co Fermanagh
Tel: 028-66325000   Fax: 028-66327342
castle@fermanagh.gov.uk   www.enniskillencastle.co.uk   HeritageISLAND
IRELAND'S VISITOR ATTRACTIONS

- Open Saturday to Monday, 2.00 to 5.00; Tuesday to Friday, 10.00 to 5.00 (closed weekends October to April, closed Sundays, May, June and September)
- Adults, £2.75; Children, £1.65; Family, £7.15
- Located in town of Enniskillen
- Caters for school groups/tours

♿ ♦♦ 🎁

Dating back to the fifteenth century, this impressive castle overlooks Lough Erne on the edge of Enniskillen. The darkened vaults show life in the castle in the fifteenth and seventeenth centuries and its history can be traced from its beginnings as a stronghold of the Maguire chieftains to its use as a barracks in the 1700s and 1800s. This popular family attraction includes displays on Fermanagh's history, wildlife and landscape with audio-visual programmes and special exhibitions featuring art, archaeology, local history and cultural heritage. Visitors may also explore the old castle keep which houses the Museum of the Royal Inniskilling Fusiliers.

Fermanagh Lakeland Forum

Broadmeadow, Enniskillen, Co Fermanagh
Tel: 028-66324121   Fax: 028-66328622
fif@fermanagh.gov.uk   www.fermanagh-online.com

- Open daily; times vary, please telephone
- Costs vary per activity; please telephone
- Located in the centre of town, beside bus station
- Caters for children's parties
- Caters for school groups/tours

Fermanagh Lakeland Forum is a first-class leisure centre with pool, squash courts, fitness centre, outdoor facilities including a huge adventure play area, indoor soft play areas and more. A new outdoor leisure facility providing a variety of activities for children and young people between the ages of eight and 16 is now available. Called "The Zone", it has a range of challenging equipment for enjoyment such as tunnels, slides, castle, jungle walk, cableway, net climber, tyre swing, ladder, basket and ordinary swing, basketball/soccer kick-about area.

Florence Court

Enniskillen, Co Fermanagh
Tel: 028-66348249   Fax: 028-66348873
florencecourt@nationaltrust.org.uk   www.nationaltrust.org.uk

- Grounds open April to September, 10.00 to 8.00; October to March, 10.00 to 4.00; House open June to August, 12.00 to 6.00 (1.00 to 6.00 in June); March 15 to May, September, weekends, 12.00 to 6.00
- Grounds: £2.50 per car; House: adults, £4.00; children, £2.00; family, £10.50
- Located eight miles SW of Enniskillen

Florence Court is a truly welcoming home. The house tour takes visitors inside the heart of the house, and as each new door opens more about the family and the staff is discovered; their fine rococo surroundings and how they lived and worked together. The house is set below the stunning backdrop of the Cuilcagh Mountains with glorious open views down to the Fermanagh lakelands. Visitors will discover many serene and beautiful corners by exploring the area. There is also a beautiful garden and a play area for children.

Marble Arch Caves European Geopark

Marlbank Scenic Loop, Florencecourt, Co Fermanagh
Tel: 028-66348855   Fax: 028-66348928
mac@fermanagh.gov.uk   www.marblearchcaves.net

HeritageISLAND
IRELAND'S VISITOR ATTRACTIONS

- Open from March to September, 10.00 to 5.00 (4.30 from March to June and in September)
- Adults, £7.00; Children, £4.00; Family, £18.00
- Caters for children's parties
- Caters for school groups/tours
- Special programmes for children

Marble Arch Caves allow visitors to explore a fascinating natural world of rivers, waterfalls, winding passages and lofty chambers. Electrically powered boats carry visitors along a subterranean river and walkways allow easy access to a bewildering variety of cave formations. An education service is available for schools with cave tours, woodland walks and field studies. The nearby Cuilcagh Mountain Park offers some of the best-preserved bog areas in Ireland. The importance of Marble Arch Caves and Cuilcagh Mountain Park has been recognised on an international scale as they were jointly awarded UNESCO Global Geopark status in 2004, one of 25 such sites around the world.

Sheelin Irish Lace Museum

Bellaneleck, Enniskillen, Co Fermanagh
Tel: 028-66348052
info@irishlacemuseum.com   www.irishlacemuseum.com

- Open Monday to Saturday, 10.00 to 6.00
- Adults, £3.00; Children, £1.00
- Located in Bellanaleck, four miles from Enniskillen

The Lace Museum, which has approximately 700 exhibits, traces the history of lace-making in Ireland and conveys to the visitor the importance of the industry to Ireland as a whole and to Irish women in particular. All the five main types of lace made in Ireland are represented in the collection — Youghal, Inishmacsaint, Crochet, Limerick and Carrickmacross. All the laces date from between 1850 and 1900. On display are several wedding gowns, veils, shawls, parasols, collars, baby bonnets, christening gowns, flounces, jackets and many more items.

Tully Castle

Derrygonnelly, Co Fermanagh
Tel: 028-90543037
www.ehsni.gov.uk/places/monuments

- Open July and August, Wednesday to Sunday, 10.00 to 6.00
- No entrance fee
- Located 4.8 km north of Derrygonnelly

These impressive remains of a fortified house and bawn are set in the beautiful Tully Point in Lower Lough Erne. It was first documented in 1619, shortly after being built for the Hume family, who lived there until 1641, when it was captured and burned by the Maguires and never re-occupied. Historically it is a "time capsule" as it was lived in for only 30 years. A seventeenth-century-style garden has been recreated for visitors to enjoy. An abandoned farmhouse, just a short stroll along a pathway from the Castle, has been restored as a Visitor Centre and contains an exhibition telling some local stories.

Monaghan County Museum

1-2 Hill Street, Monaghan
Tel: 047-82928   Fax: 047-71189
comuseum@monaghancoco.ie   www.monaghan.ie/museum

- Open Tuesday to Friday, 10.00 to 5.00; Saturday, 11.00 to 5.00 (closed 1.00 to 2.00)
- No entrance fee
- Located in Monaghan Town
- Caters for school groups/tours

Monaghan County Museum was established in 1974 to provide an education and leisure service for County Monaghan and to collect, preserve and display the heritage of the County. Archaeology, Local History, Folk life, Crafts, Transport, Coinage and Industry are among the principal areas of interest. The unique fourteenth-century Cross of Clogher and the fine collection of early medieval crannóg (lake dwelling) artefacts are among the best items in the museum. Acquisition of paintings and drawings forms part of a permanent art collection.

Aladdin's Kingdom

12 Mountjoy Road, Omagh, Co Tyrone
Tel: 028-82251550

- Open year round, Saturday, 10.30 to 6.30, Sunday 2.00 to 6.30; Monday to Friday, 2.30 to 7.00
- Contact Aladdin's Kingdom for cost information
- Caters for children's parties
- Caters for school groups/tours
- Special programmes for children

🍽 ♿ ♟

Aladdin's Kingdom is an indoor, soft play children's activity centre with features such as ball pools, slides, swings, climbing frames, rope bridges, crawl tunnels, dizzy discs and aerial gliders. Children's birthday parties and group packages are a speciality.

Barrontop Fun Farm

35 Barron Road, Donemana, Strabane, Co Tyrone
Fax/Tel: 028-71398649
barrontop@hotmail.co.uk   www.barrontop.co.uk

- Open daily July and August, 10.30 to 5.30; weekends from March 17; other times by appointment
- Adults, £3.00; Children, £3.50
- Located off the Artigarvan—Donemana road
- Caters for children's parties
- Caters for school tours
- Special programmes for children

🍽 ♿ ♟ 🎁

Barrontop Fun Farm provides a unique opportunity for children to feed, handle and see at first hand many types of animals in a farm environment. Children are able to bottle feed a lamb, stroke a calf, cuddle a rabbit or puppy or hold a newly hatched chick. They can also enjoy the rheas, pot-bellied pigs, deer and rare breeds of poultry, as well as play on the adventure playground or indoor bouncy castle or enjoy a leisurely ride on a tractor and trailer. Lots of indoor activities for wet weather.

Bog Museum

51 Dungannon road, Coalisland, Co Tyrone
Tel: 028-87749041   Fax: 028-87749041
brian@islandturfcrafts.com   www.islandturfcrafts.com

- Open 9.30 to 5.30
- Free entry
- Located at 51 Dungannon Road, Coalisland, off the A45
- Caters for school groups/tours
- Provides guided tours

The Bog Museum reconstructs the life styles and habits of prehistoric Ireland excavated from Irish Boglands. It includes old artefacts which reveal much about the rich and varied history of Ireland before and after the Ice Age. We have an indoor bog, bones and large antlers of the Great Irish Elk dating back 15,000 years and bog oak sculptures and turf products.

Gray's Printing Press

49 Main Street, Strabane, Co Tyrone
Tel: 028-71884094
www.nationaltrust.org.uk

- Open April-May and September, Saturdays 2.00 to 5.00; June, Tuesday to Saturday, 2.00 to 5.00; July-August, Tuesday to Saturday, 11.00 to 5.00
- Adults, £2.80; Children, £1.70; Family, £7.30
- Located in Strabane city centre
- Caters for school groups/tours

At Gray's Printing Press visitors can take a guided tour of the eighteenth-century printing press where John Dunlap, the printer of the American Declaration of Independence, and James Wilson, grandfather of President Woodrow Wilson, learnt their trade. There is a collection of nineteenth-century hand-printing machines, as well as an audio-visual display. The former stationer's shop is now a local museum run by Strabane District Council.

Peatlands Country Park

Derryhubbert Road, Dungannon, Co Tyrone
Tel: 028-38851102   Fax: 028-38851821
www.ehsni.gov.uk/places/parks

- Open daily from 9.00 to 9.00 Easter to September; from 9.00 to 5.00 in winter
- No entrance fee; Train prices: adults, £1.00, children, £0.50 (under-fives free)
- Located at Junction 13 off the M1
- Caters for school groups/tours

Peatlands Country Park was specifically established to promote and facilitate peatland awareness and issues. Amongst the attractions is an outdoor site where visitors can get the feel (and smell!) of cutting turf. Within the park are two National Nature Reserves, declared in 1980 for their unique flora and fauna species, many of which are found nowhere else in Northern Ireland. The Peatlands Park narrow gauge railway has been associated with the area since the 1950s and is a big attraction for the young and old alike. The new locomotive can take up to 70 passengers at a time on a 1.5 km journey through leafy tunnels and restored open bog.

Ulster American Folk Park

2 Mellon Road, Omagh, Co Tyrone
Tel: 028-82243292   Fax: 028-82242241
info@uafp.co.uk   www.folkpark.com

HeritageISLAND
IRELAND'S VISITOR ATTRACTIONS

- Open April to September, Monday to Saturday, 10.30 to 4.30; Sunday, 11.00 to 5.00; October to March, Monday to Friday, 10.30 to 3.30
- Adults, £4.50; Children, £2.50; Family, £11.50
- Located six miles outside Omagh on A5
- Caters for school groups/tours

The Ulster American Folk Park is a museum of emigration and folk life telling the story of the floods of emigrants who left these shores. Outdoor site has 26 buildings, mostly original Irish thatched and American log structures. Sail away to the new world onboard the Brig Union life-sized emigrant ship. Two complete streets on old and new world sites. Daily demonstrations include blacksmithing, spinning, printing and cookery. Costumed guides man the exhibit buildings.

Wellbrook Beetling Mill

20 Wellbrook Road, Corkhill, Cookstown, Co Tyrone
Tel: 028-86751735   Fax: 028-86751715
wellbrook@nationaltrust.org.uk   www.nationaltrust.org.uk

- Open daily July 1 to August 31, 12.00 to 6.00; March 15 to June 30, September, open weekends, 12.00 to 6.00
- Adults, £3.10; Children, £1.80; Family, £8.00
- Located four miles west of Cookstown, half a mile off Cookstown—Omagh road (A505)
- Caters for school groups/tours

Linen manufacture was of major importance in eighteenth-century Ireland and beetling was the final stage in the production process. This water-powered hammer mill has its original machinery, still in working order, and there is a "hands-on" demonstration of how linen was manufactured in the nineteenth century, which is popular with children. The mill is situated in an attractive glen through which there are many good walks.

Heritage Outlook is a magazine that celebrates Ireland's natural and built heritage.

Produced biannually by the Heritage Council, Heritage Outlook is the only national magazine that focuses on all aspects of Irish heritage.

Heritage Outlook is a full-colour 32-page modern magazine with vibrant and varied content. Its extensive readership is diverse and influential, and includes professionals working in the heritage field, state departments, local authorities, non-governmental organisations, community groups, journalists, teachers and academics. Heritage Outlook is for anyone who has an interest in preserving Ireland's heritage. It carries news, provides analysis and offers thought-provoking articles on all aspects of heritage.

Heritage is defined as including the following areas:

- *Archaeological objects;*
- *Heritage Gardens & Parks;*
- *Architectural Heritage;*
- *Flora & Fauna;*
- *Wildlife Habitats;*
- *Landscapes;*
- *Monuments;*
- *Geology;*
- *Seascapes & wrecks;*
- *Inland Waterways*

If you would like to receive a copy of Heritage Outlook please email: mail@heritagecouncil.com

Kilkenny, Ireland. Telephone: +353 56 7770777. Fax: +353 56 7770788.
www.heritagecouncil.ie

Index by Activity

Adventure Centres and Fun Parks

Castles, Stately Homes and Gardens

Caves

Heritage Centres and National Monuments

Museums, Galleries and Arts Centres

National Parks, Forest Parks and Nature Reserves

Open Farms

Outdoor and Water Sports

Zoos, Aquariums, Pet Farms and Wildlife

Index by Name of Organisation

(names in **bold** are new to this edition

Listing Form for Next Edition of *FOR THE KIDS3! A Family-Friendly Guide to Outings and Activities in Ireland for Children*

To be included in the next edition of the directory at <u>no cost</u>, please fill out this form and return it to the address below or send the information by e-mail to dgivens@theliffeypress.com. Please also send us a suitable photograph (or high resolution jpeg) of your facilities to use next to your listing in the directory.

Name of Organisation:_____

Address: _____

_____

Tel: _____ Fax: _____

E-mail: _____ Web: _____

Contact Person: _____

Dates and opening hours: _____

Entrance and other fees:_____

Location and directions: _____

Description of activities and facilities (100-150 words — please focus in particular on ones aimed specifically at children):_____

_____

_____

_____

_____

_____

_____

Please tick if you have:

☐ Coffee shop, restaurant

☐ Facilities for the physically disabled

☐ Gift shop

☐ Public toilets

Please tick if your organisation:

☐ Caters for children's parties

☐ Caters for school groups/tours

☐ Has special programmes for children

Please return <u>with a suitable photo(s)</u> to The Liffey Press, Ashbrook House, 10 Main Street, Raheny, Dublin 5. Tel: (01) 851-1458. E-mail: dgivens@theliffeypress.com